Interpreting Diana

Television Audiences and the Death of a Princess

Robert Turnock

 Publishing

For Jean and Kirsty Turnock, and Robert Carnie

First published in 2000 by the
British Film Institute
21 Stephen Street, London W1P 2LN

The British Film Institute is the UK national agency with responsibility for
encouraging the arts of film and television and conserving them in the national
interest.

Set by Ketchup
Printed in Great Britain by Cromwell Press, United Kingdom

Cover designed by Ketchup
Cover image: Floral tributes at Kensington Palace (Tony Kyriacou/Rex Features)

British Library Cataloguing-in-Publication Data
A catalogue record for this book is available from the British Library
ISBN 0–85170–788–2 (hb)
ISBN 0–85170–789–0 (pb)

Contents

Acknowledgments

This book has been a long time coming and has probably exhausted much credit and goodwill. My thanks go to a significant number of people. In particular, I am grateful to Janet Willis and Richard Paterson at the BFI. Not only did they set up and run the original Audience Tracking Study project along with Duncan Petrie, but they bravely agreed to initiate this project at short notice as well. They were also a constant source of help and guidance while I first studied and then worked at the BFI.

I would also like to extend a big thank you to friends and colleagues who worked, at various stages, in the Centre for Audience and Industry Research and the Television and Projects Unit at the BFI. These were Mike Allen, Jacintha Cusack, Alice Dudley, Mark Duguid, Ilja Gregory, Rachel Hughes, Kathleen Luckey, Nick Pettigrew and Elaine Sheppard. Honorary drinking members also included Jim Barratt, Hannah Davies, Dick Fiddy and Kate Stables. My thanks go to all of them, and to others engaged in television and educational work at the BFI, for providing a stimulating, supportive and fun environment for research. In particular, I would like to acknowledge Alison Preston for her advice and support over the years, especially during the darker days of writing, and Veronica Taylor for her support during the darker days generally.

Appreciation is also due to David Gauntlett and Annette Hill, for ably demonstrating that it was possible to make sense of the mass of complex Audience Tracking Study data, and again to Annette for her advice and reading of various drafts. Another deserving of important mention is David Morrison at the University of Leeds, for his advice, understanding and tolerance while I finished this project.

I would like to offer my many thanks to Nick Couldry for his reading of later drafts. His insightful and supportive comments have been invaluable in helping me to complete this book. Where I have not adopted his suggestions, I have done so at my own peril. What follows is solely my responsibility. My supreme gratitude must be reserved for Andrew Lockett at BFI Publishing, for his tireless encouragement of this project from the outset. That this book was ever finished is in no small part thanks to him.

In the end, of course, recognition and gratitude must be extended to the Tracking Study respondents who took the time and trouble to complete and return their diary–questionnaires in this special one-off project.

Introduction

The premature death of the Princess of Wales in Paris in the early hours of Sunday 31 August 1997 signalled the dramatic start to a week characterised by intense media activity and high 'public' emotion. On the day that the princess died, non-stop live news dominated television screens as presenters and pundits relayed, replayed and speculated on the details of the accident and its consequences, while outside links brought pictures of the initial crowds starting to converge around London palaces. Throughout the rest of the week, the apparently 'unprecedented' displays of public grief continued to provide one of the major news narratives as television and the press brought extraordinary pictures of crowds queuing for hours to sign condolence books and tearful mourners laying flowers. These images, read as evidence of 'public' mourning and of Diana's popularity, fuelled criticism of the royal family for its apparent cold-hearted neglect of the princess when she was alive, and for being out of touch with the wave of 'public' sympathy after her death. On Saturday 6 September, the week's media frenzy drew to a close with the princess's funeral service, televised to around 32 million people in the United Kingdom[1] and to an enormous global audience.

In the wake of these dramatic scenes, the British Film Institute (BFI) contacted members of its television Audience Tracking Study to find out how they responded to the news and the television coverage that week. The findings of this research form the basis of this book. Before looking at what respondents had to say about these events and what this entails, there are a few housekeeping points.

The Audience Tracking Study

The BFI's Audience Tracking Study was set up in 1990 to follow the lives and viewing habits of a sample of people over a five-year period. The initiative followed the success of the BFI's mass obser-vation-style project *One Day in the Life of Television*. More than 20,000 people took part in the original ODILOT project, including viewers and television practitioners. Each person volunteered in response to promotion in the press and on television, and submitted a detailed diary of what they did and watched on 1 November 1988.[2] The sample for the Audience Tracking Study was drawn from par-ticipants of this original project, with around 750 viewers selected to represent, as accurately as possible, the diversity of the television audience in the United Kingdom on the basis of age, social class, gen-der, marital status and household composition. Of this number, around 500 agreed to participate in the five-year study. The data col-lection ran from 1991 to 1996 and, at the end of this period, the BFI had retained, through careful management and administration, around 450 respondents who had regularly participated in the pro-ject. Although the sample was deemed representative, its self-selecting nature meant that there *was* a skewing of the sample towards both middle-class and more mature viewers. Unfortunately, there were hardly any respondents from ethnic communities.

The study itself took the form of special questionnaire–diaries which were sent to respondents three times a year over the five-year project period. Each diary asked respondents to comment on the same day's viewing. Combining both open-ended qualitative ques-tions with tick-box–type quantitative questions, the diaries sought to extract information about the types of programme viewed, who they were viewed with, how viewing was planned and how it fitted in with the rest of the day's activities. Annual update questionnaires sought to keep abreast of personal and household changes to examine view-ing patterns within the context of both daily life and life change. Throughout the five-year period, respondents experienced a range of significant life changes including leaving school, changing jobs, unemployment, retirement, marriage, divorce and bereavement. The long-term nature of the project also permitted the revision of ques-tions to investigate issues that emerged either from the data or as a reflection of public concern or interest. Special questions focused, for example, on the popularity of programmes with medical themes and on the television news coverage of the conflict in former Yugoslavia. The project's initial findings were published as *Television and the Household* (Petrie and Willis, 1995) and the main research findings as *TV Living: Television, Culture and Everyday Life* (Gauntlett and Hill, 1999).

The Death of Diana

In the wake of the extraordinary scenes of mass grieving and the extended television coverage of both the breaking news story and the princess's funeral, the BFI decided to contact the original Tracking Study respondents to canvass them on their views and opinions of the television coverage that week. The motivation was twofold: a simple spirit of enquiry and the desire to capture actual audience responses to the television coverage of this historic event for posterity.

The idea and decision to undertake this opportunistic project was made in the days following the princess's funeral. To try to capture responses to the event while they were still fresh in people's memories, a special one-off qualitative questionnaire was devised, printed and mailed out to the remaining 450 BFI respondents within two-and-a-half days. The questionnaire itself was broken down into four sections. The first concentrated on the Sunday the news broke. It asked about how, where and when people heard the news of the princess's death, how they reacted to the news, whether they watched the continuous television coverage that day and what they thought about it. The second section asked various questions about their responses to the television coverage in the following week. It asked where respondents obtained their information, whether they had participated in the public displays of mourning and what influence television had on their views, feelings and actions. The third section looked at responses to the television coverage of the funeral and asked about how the funeral was watched, with whom and what respondents thought about it. The fourth asked more general questions about the overall impact of the week's events, such as whether or not respondents felt the princess's death had affected them personally, and asked respondents to add any other comments they wanted.

In all, 278 qualitative questionnaires were returned to the BFI, a substantial number considering that the sample had lain dormant for around eighteen months. This sample does, however, present some problems. As we have seen above, the nature of the original sample was self-selecting, providing a bias towards an older, more middle-class demographic. The questionnaires returned in the wake of the princess's death also reflected this skewing. There was also a slight bias towards women, with a 3:2 ratio of women to men. As previously observed, there were no members of ethnic minorities. It should also be noted here that the self-selecting nature of the sample might also have meant that respondents attracted to participating had a particular interest in watching television. This, combined with the fact that older viewers are the biggest watchers of television (Midwinter, 1991), *might* have meant that there was a higher exposure to the Diana coverage amongst Tracking Study respondents than viewers generally. As a result of these factors, this book makes *no* claims towards representativeness of a wider UK public.

Nonetheless, given the in-depth qualitative nature of the replies of BFI respondents, the philosophy behind this book – as the title *Interpreting Diana* suggests – lies more within a hermeneutic tradition of interpretation and understanding than on a statistical assessment of group behaviour. *Some* of the findings *have* been based on crude or bald statistics, but this is where the relative numbers involved clearly signify a definite separation between audience responses and where they suggest a variety of social behaviours and processes. Graham Murdock has previously warned about the obfuscation of numbers and statistics in cultural studies projects, whereby vague and imprecise quantifying (such as the use of words 'some' and 'many') can perhaps lead to unjustifiable or unverifiable claims (1997). Given the unrepresentative nature and size of the sample here, however, precision in quantification would have been spurious and, as a result, some vagueness in the description of numbers remains a necessary evil of this project.

The nature also of qualitative research, with its stress on the way that people think and feel, can also fragment study samples and emphasise diversity of opinion. Yet the fragmentation of opinion in this sample is significant *exactly* because it highlights a range of responses and interpretations. Given that the media rhetoric in the period following the princess's death emphasised 'public' unity, and given that much previous study of mass media has tended to homogenise its audience, this emphasis on diversity of opinion takes on a singularly important resonance. That the project sample may be skewed does not undermine the results, therefore, because exegesis, interpretation and understanding are based on the range of responses and processes involved, rather than on statistical weighting. Where respondents' quotations have been used, these have been selected simply on the basis that they best articulate and exemplify that range of responses and processes. To provide these respondents with some 'colour', they have been accompanied by details of gender and age, for example (M30).

Furthermore, while the examination of audience responses here involves a hermeneutic process, this is not to say that it belies sophistry or is caught in the rhetorical trap of the hermeneutic circle where understanding is predicated on anticipated, or *prejudiced*, findings. Undertaken at short notice in response to both the extraordinary television output and the extraordinary scenes of 'public' participation, the project was not motivated by theoretical concerns or questions. Part of the aim was simply to throw light on some of the events of that week and to assess television's role in those events. Given that the BFI had previously established a long-term relationship with these respondents, it was felt that they would be able to provide articulate and frank accounts of their views and feelings about the television coverage that week.

In any event, the Princess of Wales was a complex and contradictory character when alive, and the media and audience responses to her death were no less complex or contradictory. As a result, the analysis here of respondents' replies has employed a process much akin to *bricolage*, where available theories in communications, media and cultural studies, sociology and social anthropology have been employed. The effectiveness of this strategy will be for the reader to judge. Nonetheless, it is evident that no study of this sort can ever fully account for the media and 'public' phenomena in the days following the princess's death. This book can only therefore hope to make a modest contribution to a larger debate.

The Arrangement of this Book

What follows is broken down into five chapters. The first deals with how people reacted to the breaking news on the morning of Sunday 31 August 1997. It goes on to look at how television responded to the crisis and how audience members reacted to the coverage. The second chapter examines why people were upset by the princess's death. This is an extremely complex area, but, as most people had never met her and only 'knew' her through the media, it examines ways in which television constructs characters and narratives, and contributes to people's knowledge of the world. The third chapter looks at the extent of 'public' mourning for Diana. It questions the media rhetoric of 'unity in grief', looks at how people have previously responded to public tragedy and explores how television may have helped construct mourning spaces and an apparent public unity. The fourth chapter looks at audience behaviour and responses to the princess's funeral on Saturday 6 September 1997, and assesses the usefulness of various perspectives through which to understand this event. The first three chapters end with a brief summary of points and findings, while the funeral chapter ends with a broader discussion of the ambiguous nature of the event. The final chapter, therefore, does not in any way constitute a restatement of findings or conclusions. Rather it consists of some final thoughts regarding the complex relationship between television and social processes in the week the Princess of Wales died.

Notes

1. 'Overnight Ratings', *Broadcast*, 12 September 1997.
2. For details of the ODILOT project see S. Day-Lewis, *One Day in the Life of Television* (London: Grafton Books, 1989).

1
The Breaking News

Ever since the assassination of J. F. Kennedy in Dallas on 22 November 1963, it has become a cliché of popular memory and journalism to recall where you were when you heard that an historic event had occurred or that someone important had died. Yet asking BFI Audience Tracking Study respondents where, when and how they heard the news of Diana's death reveals a lot about their immediate reactions, long before anyone can start making suggestions about media influence and a media-led public response. At the same time, it also allows us to look at what people did next and provides an insight into media use, both at times of potential crisis and tragedy, as well as in everyday life.

It would appear from responses of members of the Tracking Study that the morning of 31 August 1997 started just like any other Sunday. People were going about their normal weekend business. Some were sleeping in, recovering from a hard week at work or hard partying the night before. Some were up early doing household chores, getting ready to go to church or, in some cases, preparing to go to work. At the end of summer, some were packing to go on holiday or take a day trip, or planning to relax in the garden. At this time of the weekend, media audiences were perhaps at their most fragmented. As a result, the news of this extraordinary event filtered into homes at different times of the morning.

In the majority of cases, it was radio which alerted people to the news. Strategically located around the household – in the bedroom, bathroom and kitchen – the radio is most often used as a background to other activities such as getting up and preparing for the day ahead.

With some BBC national radio stations playing sombre music and others providing unscheduled news services, many people switching on their radios were already disorientated by not finding their normal Sunday programmes. Once they made sense of what they were hearing, initial incomprehension turned to shock, with many instantly feeling tearful, as the following two respondents suggest:

> *I was asleep when I heard the news on my radio alarm clock. I heard 'whales dead' and pictured the sea creatures. 'The car crash', 'Paris'. I was confused, what were they doing out of the sea? Then I was wide awake and stunned as I realised what had happened. I cried as I told my children the news; they were all upset, too.* (F37)

> *On Sunday 31 August, we put on radio at 7.55 a.m., only to hear about Princess Diana being talked about in the past tense. The 8 a.m. News on Radio 4 told us the awful truth – that she was dead. I couldn't believe it to begin with. The fact that she had been killed in a car crash made it seem even worse and pointless. What an awful end to such a lovely woman. I cried – I couldn't help it.* (F45)

One woman heard the news on her car radio and had to pull over because she felt so tearful. Others rushed to tell family or other household members. Indeed, for those who took part in the BFI study, hearing the news from friends or family, either in person or by telephone, came second to the radio in how people learned of the tragedy.

> *My daughter rang me at 8.45 a.m. to tell me the news because she knew that I do not put my TV or radio on in the morning. I turned the TV on and woke my partner; I was crying, I could not believe it.* (F54)

As a result of the fragmented radio audience and the word-of-mouth diffusion of news, it was only one in five who first learned of her death through television. Those who turned on the television on Sunday morning did so to have it on as background or to watch a specific programme, such as a weather report, or in some cases turned it on later in the day expecting to see a favourite soap opera:

> *I didn't learn of the tragedy until just before 1 o'clock. I switched on for the* EastEnders *omnibus and saw Nelson Mandela offering condolences. I immediately thought Prince Philip or the Queen Mum had died. The shock when Martyn Lewis announced it was Diana who was dead was enormous, and the details only emerged over the next half-hour. I immediately rang my best friend, but she had heard the news in the early hours of the morning. It affected my day, as it did everyone else's day, with great emotion and disbelief.* (F55)

In one instance, a woman did not learn of the accident until 6 p.m., when she turned the television on for the early evening news.

In any event, when respondents did hear the news of Diana's death, many rushed to their televisions for more information. For many, this was to confirm the news they simply could not believe. As one respondent (F38) suggested: 'My nine-year-old son woke me at 8.45 and said "Princess Diana is dead." I rushed to the TV because I didn't believe him. I immediately filled with immense emotion, tears, disbelief.' Others automatically valued television over other forms of media. Another respondent (F32) noted: 'I couldn't believe it! I thought it was a cruel joke (seeing that Diana had had such a bad press recently). I thought if it is on television then it must be true.'

Yet it should also be noted that not everyone shared the initial sense of shock as expressed by some of the respondents above. Some members of the audience were surprised, but did not necessarily express the same sense of shock; some respondents were simply not interested from the outset, displaying a cynical understanding of how this would come to dominate output in the days ahead:

> *My first thought and statement was to the effect that 'This is all we'll get for the next week, then' and that it would hardly be worth getting daily papers or watching TV or listening to the radio, as the subject would completely oversee all other events.* (M44)

These responses reveal a number of things. First is the level of shock experienced by the Tracking Study respondents. As we have seen, some respondents reacted with shock, disbelief and tears; in a quantitative assessment of how people responded, at least 40 per cent said that they were shocked or shattered on hearing the news.[1] The significance of this initial shock and disbelief is that it constitutes a spontaneous response to the news and prefigures the extended media coverage of the event and the apparent scenes of 'public' mourning. On the one hand, this sense of shock constitutes evidence of a disruption to normality; on the other, it *potentially* signifies an early indication of a grief reaction to the princess's death. As sociologists and psychologists recorded in the wake of the Kennedy assassination, for example, first reactions included shock and disbelief on hearing the news (Schramm, 1965; Mindak and Hursch, 1965; Sheatsley and Feldman, 1965). As Sheatsley and Feldman go on to argue, after Engel (1961), such a reaction is a common first stage of the grieving process.

Whether or not BFI respondents experienced grief will be explored fully in the next chapter. This initial shock and disbelief, however, also accounts for why people wanted to share the news with others. This rapid spread of news by face-to-face communication or telephone is accounted for, Sheatsley and Feldman suggest, by the profound need of members of the public to talk about these events. In their study of reactions to the death of J. F. Kennedy, they found that more than half of the US public had felt the urge to pass on the information quickly. This explains why almost half of the American public learned the news direct from others (Sheatsley and Feldman, 1965). Part of this urge is people's need to seek reassurance from those around them that things are going to be okay. When people are uncertain, they look for cues from others about how to behave, and this is equally true in grief (Walter, 1999a). Yet what Mindak and Hursch (1965) suggest in their survey in the wake of the Kennedy assassination is that people did not, in the last instance, have faith in or believe their friends, relatives or associates:

In sudden disruptions of the environment, people tend to look to other people for information that will reduce anxiety by verifying their knowledge. In this case, almost all of those who heard about the assassination from another person did not believe the news until they had confirmed it themselves by hearing it from radio or television.
(p. 132)

Mindak and Hursch found that, where available, people turned to television rather than radio for news and information. While they do not discuss why this was so, we might be able to speculate that in a world dominated by the visual, as a medium involving moving images, sound and colour, television has more authority than radio. What is certainly the case, on a daily basis, is that more people obtain their news from television than newspapers or radio (Independent Television Commission, 1997) and that Tracking Study respondents in particular are regular and habitual consumers of television news (Gauntlett and Hill, 1999). Furthermore, in their study of daily news consumption amongst Tracking Study respondents, Gauntlett and Hill concurred with John Corner (1995), who has argued that public confidence in television is partly dependent on the viewer being able to *see* events and persons for themselves. In their examination of viewer responses to the coverage of the Bosnian conflict on television, Gauntlett and Hill found that certain images left a lasting imprint in the memories of Tracking Study respondents, which they attribute to what Corner describes as 'picture power'. Corner argues that 'when sufficiently strong in revelatory/dramatic character such picturing may serve to crystallise the whole report and to enter public circulation with a force no other form of contemporary journalism could possess' (1995, p. 61).

Yet, as will be discussed in more detail further below, television confers legitimacy and authority on news presenters. Combined with the aesthetics of news broadcasting which creates close bonds between presenter and viewer, these newsreaders carry claims to 'truth' which command the trust and respect of people watching. As a result, television news constitutes a trusted and respected source of information, the need for which is heightened at moments of crisis and anxiety.

What is clear is that most of these people were not initially watching television on a Sunday morning; it was simply not part of their weekend routines. For many people, Sunday can be just as busy or hectic as any other day of the week, but the suggestion that 'nothing ever happens on a Sunday' retains some residual truth when thinking about the news. While the mechanics of government, economy and legal system occupy the news during the week, there is often little in the way of 'hard news' at the weekend. In the print media, while the tabloids still chase the salacious and titillating (scandal never being confined to the weekday), the broadsheets are more occupied with 'think-pieces' and features, and complemented by the burgeoning lifestyle sections focusing on the arts, sport, gardening, travel and so on. That the weekend is not expected to yield much in the way of 'hard news' is evidenced by the fact that most papers 'go to bed' relatively early on a Saturday evening. On the morning of 31 August 1997, details of the accident emerged too late to feature in most editions of the Sunday press. As a respondent (M50) noted ironically, 'Anyone who followed the news only from the newspaper early editions could have had a carefree day.'

The Television Response

Many people did rush to their television sets to verify the news or to try to obtain more information. Yet what did they see when they got there? The news broke on the BBC at 5.15 on the morning of 31 August, when Nik Gowing on BBC World, being transmitted on BBC 1 and BBC 2, announced:

> This is BBC Television from London. A short while ago, Buckingham
> Palace confirmed the death of Diana, Princess of Wales. (*Ariel*,
> 2 September 1997, p. 4).

With those words began on the BBC and ITV channels what Tamar Liebes describes as 'marathonic' broadcasting (1998). Day-long coverage dominated television screens as well-known presenters, some close to tears, relayed and replayed details of the princess's death. Over the day, live news reported new developments. Initial crowds and flowers outside London palaces were covered; reactions were sought from members of the public; broadcast journalists waited outside Balmoral for the royal family to leave for church, hoping perhaps for some official or personal statement; Prime Minister Tony Blair's statement from outside his church in his Sedgefield constituency was shown; official reactions were gathered from other senior politicians, party and world leaders; the statement made by Earl Spencer, Diana's brother, was televised from outside his home in South Africa, where he indicted the press for having 'blood on their hands'; the departure of Prince Charles and Diana's two sisters to collect her body from Paris was followed; and the return of her body to the United Kingdom in the early evening was broadcast. Much studio time was spent on speculation: the causes of the accident; her romance with Dodi Al Fayed; the implications for press regulation; and the repercussions for the royal family. Interviews were held with people who had known the princess or who had worked with her on charitable projects.

Normal scheduling on the two main terrestrial channels, BBC 1 and ITV, was abandoned and the day was given over to live and continuous news. BBC 2 simulcast with BBC 1 until 3 p.m. when it ran a revised schedule of programmes including *Sunday Grandstand* and factual and documentary programmes such as a popular travelogue with Michael Palin and a natural history programme. BBC 1 stayed with the Diana coverage throughout the day. At 6.30 p.m., a special church service was televised live from St Paul's Cathedral in the traditional Sunday BBC 1 *Songs of Praise* 'God slot'. This programme was being transmitted when the aircraft carrying the Princess of Wales's body arrived at RAF Northolt outside London. The decision to show scenes of airmen carrying Diana's coffin from the aircraft overplayed with the singing of 'Psalm 130' ('Out of the deep have I called unto thee, O' Lord) produced what has been described as 'one of the most remarkable television effects of the whole week' (Davie and Martin, 1999, p. 188). This was followed throughout the evening by tribute programmes such as *Diary of a Princess* and *Diana – A Tribute*. The non-stop coverage on BBC 1 finally ended at 12.30 a.m. the following morning, when it returned to its overnight BBC World News service. ITV ran live non-stop coverage from *GMTV* in the morning right throughout the day until 7.30 p.m., when it showed the regular edition of the popular soap *Coronation Street*, followed by the popular drama *Heartbeat*, an extended hour-long news programme and then the popular Napoleonic drama *Sharpe*.

Channel 4 ran a news programme for more than three hours on the Sunday morning, but then returned to a more or less normal schedule with news updates between each programme, and ran an extended news programme for an hour in the evening. Channel 5, which had commenced transmission only a few months earlier, ran short news updates regularly between normal programming that Sunday.

Television as Comforter

As we have suggested, at times of crisis people automatically turn to their television sets and this was certainly the case when the news about Diana broke. They do this because they cannot believe what they have heard from friends or family, and in some cases even from the radio. Those who rushed to their televisions, or those turning on casually, were met with extensive blanket coverage of this extraordinary event on the three main terrestrial channels. For many respondents, the extensive coverage was not only necessary because Diana had been so important, but also because television actually demonstrated *how* important she was.

> *The fact that the networks responded by putting the news of her death before previously scheduled television showed the importance and relevance of what had happened.* (F38)

As Paul Lazarsfeld and Robert Merton argue in their discussion of mass communications and the relationship with organised social action: 'The mass media confer status on public issues, persons and organizations, and social movements' (1972, p. 497). Simply put, an important person on television becomes important by virtue of their appearance on television. As another respondent (F16) noted, 'It mirrored the importance of the event and the public's need for information.' This need for information, which Schramm (1965) and Barber (1965) both recorded following Kennedy's death, had several elements. It is partly an explanation of the hows and whys of the event, a need for reassurance that things are going to be 'okay', and for reassurance that individual viewer responses are not inappropriate. The following two respondents, for example, note this profound need for information at these different levels.

> ... that day felt different and unreal. All we wanted to do was watch the television and to be kept informed of events. We wanted to see her, despite the pain it caused. We prayed for her, but ultimately we hoped to hear that it was some dreadful mistake – but sadly it was not to be. (F24)

> I'm not that keen on Martyn Lewis, but he was there, serious, dependable, shaken but not stirred. I felt I needed him. We did need to be told all the details about how, when and if possible why. We needed the television to stay with us all day, going over all the questions. I was so relieved to find I was not alone. My reactions and hurt was obviously the same as millions of others – she deserved no less and it helped to share the grief. (F48)

As this last respondent indicated, there was a need to understand how and why this had happened, which Schramm refers to as the need for an interpretation of events. Mary Anne Doane (1990) argues that certain types of 'catastrophe' such as plane crashes undermine the whole way of life for societies dependent on science and technology, and there is a need to ascribe the event to some kind of rational cause. Normality is under threat or has ceased to exist. There is, therefore, an apparent need to know how and why such an event could take place. In the end, it seems much less traumatic to lay the blame on individuals, such as the pilot, the designer or the mechanic, than accept that such arbitrary events could potentially happen to any of us (ibid.). As Schramm (1965) points out in relation to J. F. Kennedy's death, the flow of news and the ascription of the assassination to a lone, crazed gunman meant that rumours and fears of a conspiracy were quickly smothered. 'The people got the full news, they got it fast, and they got it, with a very few exceptions, accurately' (ibid., p. 22). On such occasions, Liebes argues, 'when the leader's assassin is caught and the murder is declared as the act of one "mad" individual, journalism can relax into the "priestly" mode' (1998, p. 74). However, as Liebes adds, 'The less possible it is to point to the actual villain, the less chance of a satisfactory solution, and the more powerful the role of television in providing the framing.' Where there is little in the way of new information or hard evidence, television can respond only by giving air time to speculation.

So, when Diana was killed in a pointless and sordid car accident, there was a need to find some explanation as to why it happened. In the absence of hard evidence, the need of live television to provide instantaneous, up-to-the minute information and the need to break new stories meant that early rumour and supposition about the role of the paparazzi was reported. These initial reports on the morning of the accident stirred a storm of outrage at the role of the tabloid press. This outrage gathered momentum as people outside palaces hurled abuse at photographers and reporters; Earl Spencer, the princess's brother, was televised live from outside his home in South Africa indicting newspaper proprietors by suggesting:

> ... I always believed the press would kill her in the end. But not even I could imagine that they would take such a direct hand in her death as seems to be the case.

This then became one of the main news narratives of the day. Yet, for some of the Tracking Study respondents, the immediate reporting of information regardless of whether it had been verified was an important aspect of the news that day, even if some information was later discounted or disproved:

> *They appeared to communicate news to the audience as it came to them which at times was later contradicted. Normally this would have annoyed me but on this occasion I felt I needed some information rather than none.* (F38)

As the following respondent goes on to note, however, there was actually little in the way of new information. Diana was dead and there was very little extra to report about the accident itself other than speculation about the causes and official reactions. For this respondent, the replaying of details was crucial to help her come to terms with the event:

> *The excellent broadcasters strung minimal information together and explained each point to us which we needed as we couldn't think for ourselves.* (F16)

The search for an explanation, a cause or a culprit, the need to attribute blame, continued to constitute a major news narrative in the days ahead.

Of those who took part in the Tracking Study survey, 47 per cent claimed to have found the 'marathonic' coverage on that day appropriate and justified. Indeed, there was much overall praise for the broadcasters. One respondent (M76) noted, 'The coverage was up to the best tradition of the BBC and ITV.' What was particularly notable about many of the Tracking Study responses, however, was the way in which praise was often personalised, with particular individuals (predominantly from the BBC) being singled out for commendation:

> *Standing out was Martyn Lewis … and Jenny* [sic] *Bond, called on holiday from Devon and doing a first class job.* (F61)

Martyn Lewis and Peter Scissons were superb – but Jenny [sic] Bond
really stands out from the studio presenters. She was controlled, calm
and candid. A brilliant professional tour de force. (F50)

The coverage seemed very comprehensive and I was aware of the hard
work going on in the background under what must have been very
difficult circumstances. The thing that stands out particularly is the length
each of the presenters spent on screen during the day, especially Jennie
Bond. (F53)

While Martyn Lewis was the main BBC TV anchorman in the morning, with Peter Scissons in the afternoon, the mention of Jennie Bond
stems from the fact that she was on the BBC for seventeen hours
from 6.30 a.m. to 11.40 p.m.[2] Not only did Bond report and com-
mentate on events, but also, as someone who had spoken with the
princess on numerous occasions, she was able to combine a personal
and professional perspective on the tragedy.

  The reference to the particular presenters and reporters here is
significant for revealing elements of the relationship between news
presenter and audience member in the news viewing experience.
Indeed, as we have seen previously, some respondents rushed to the
television to have news of the princess's death confirmed. As Mar-
garet Morse has argued, the authority and truth claims of television
news lie in part with the charisma and authority of the newsreader.
News personalities, for Morse, are charismatic individuals who seem
to know all the facts. They are able to link disparate stories, frag-
ments and clips into a coherent whole, thereby being 'able
spontaneously to place information in a generally valid value system'
(Morse, 1986, p. 58). What that means is that they are able to make
coherence, stability and order out of a fragmented and chaotic world.
John Ellis has suggested, in comparing the relationship between
news programmes and television soap operas, that news presenters
themselves are like soap opera characters whose regular appearance
constitutes a sense of normality (1982). At the same time, as Morse
goes on to argue – and this is certainly the case with the example of

Jennie Bond given above – regular newscasters are attractive individuals who have integrity. This is because they 'must be seen as a subject, one who "speaks the truth as he sees it" with inner conviction; otherwise, he would lack the charisma required for the impression of credibility' (Morse, 1986, p. 59).

What is also interesting is the way in which Tracking Study respondents had previously discussed television in terms of providing company, like having people in the same room as them, and often referring to certain newsreaders and presenters as friends (Gauntlett and Hill, 1999). As Morse suggests, drawing on the work of Berger and Luckmann (1967), the face-to-camera address of the news presenter re-creates that most important social experience – the face-to-face encounter. Combined with the sense of 'shared space', the direct gaze between the broadcaster and viewer, the sense of shared time, simultaneous transmission and reception, and the 'signs that the speaking subject is speaking for himself, sincerely' (Morse: 1986: 62), the impression of the presenter actually 'being there' with the viewer creates and sustains a para-social relationship (Horton and Wohl, 1956). Furthermore, newsreaders can also provide, ordinarily, a barrier between the viewer and an unsafe world (Morse, 1986). These 'trusted friends', in talking directly to the reporter at the scene on our behalf or providing a parent-like guidance to the next filmed report such as 'Some viewers might find these scenes disturbing', can mediate and mitigate upsetting and distressing information.

In the wake of the princess's death, however, the presence of visibly upset or solemn newsreaders may have eroded that aesthetic of distanciation to draw the viewer closer into a personal, subjective experience. While this may have made the television coverage more emotive, as will be discussed in the next section, the important point here is that it may have legitimated the distressed and emotional responses of some viewers. As we have observed, at times of insecurity or uncertainty, people turn to others for cues or for reassurance as to how to behave or feel. Following Diana's death, therefore, the presence of upset newsreaders contributed to a sense of shared experience, which several respondents referred to with comments such as: 'There was a feeling that we were sharing the horrors of the tragedy with the presenters' (F53) and 'The shock of everyone was obvious. I thought this was good, I needed to feel that the news-readers were affected as everybody else' (F31). For many, this was a validation of their own feelings and experiences, and a further con-firmation of the princess's importance.

It was not only the reactions of journalists or presenters which pro-vided this validation. As the day wore on, tributes poured in from senior politicians, personalities, celebrities and people who had met and worked with Diana, as well as the vox pop held outside the London palaces and the images of people laying flowers.

> *Tony Blair's contribution was spot on and set me blubbering again. I just sat with a box of tissues, nodding in agreement and sniffing.* (F48)

> *Hearing other people interviewed during the day was moving. I already admired Princess Diana so hearing such wonderful tributes was a comfort to me personally.* (F38)

Not only did television institutionally sanction Diana's death as something important, but also the appearance of members from dif-ferent levels of the establishment and the depiction of a broad sweep of the public (with particular emphasis on young people, gays and blacks) offered some reassurance to those upset at home that their emotions were not aberrant.

As we have seen, many rushed to their televisions for confirma-tion of the news of Diana's death, for more information, for an interpretation of why this had taken place and/or for reassurance that others were feeling and responding in the same way. For those who were satisfied with the extensive and empathetic coverage, it would appear that television was able to provide some degree of comfort in whichever of these ways was most important for each viewer. Nonetheless, as we shall see in the next section, not everyone was in agreement.

Television, Extension, Emotion and Emphasis

In response to the BFI's special questionnaire, just over half of respondents recorded being unhappy with the television coverage in some way. Around 20 per cent of all respondents were deeply critical of the coverage, arguing that it was 'over-the-top' and went on for too long. The remainder of the sample, however, had more mixed feelings. Some were deeply upset about Diana's death, but felt that aspects of the coverage compounded their distress in some way, or they were appalled by the 'rent-a-quotes' wheeled out for the occasion or were critical of what they saw as media hypocrisy. Some felt that there was too much coverage, with disinterested viewers complaining about the total disruption to the schedules and upset respondents craving some kind of relief from the emotion-heavy broadcast output.

In the first instance, some respondents were appalled by the way in which the television schedules were completely disrupted to cover the breaking story:

> *What is so disturbing about television is the way they think everyone is obliged to think as they do, so they calmly chop off programmes willy-nilly and so control what the public sees and said public has no say in the matter.* (F81)

While Lazarsfeld and Merton (1972) are right to suggest that television can confer status, prestige or importance to an event or a person, its ability to do this is not always uncritically received. There are those members of the public who will hold alternative or oppositional positions. Some respondents suggested this when being critical of the way the BBC broadcast the same output on BBC 1 and BBC 2:

> *I didn't consider the changes to the channels' output to be entirely justified. Why, in particular, have exactly the same broadcast on both BBC 1 and BBC 2 when something 'alternative' to the story could have been shown for a bit of light relief, even if only other news were shown. I*

*know the BBC is supposed to be the nation's broadcaster, but this was
pushing it a bit too far.* (M20)

As previously indicated, the television coverage on BBC 1 and ITV
on Sunday 31 August 1997, and on BBC 2 earlier that same day, has
much in common with what Tamar Liebes (1998) describes as a 'disaster marathon'. Liebes's account of 'disaster marathons' is based on
the television coverage which followed a series of terrorist bus
bombings in Israel in March 1996. In the wake of these incidents,
Israeli television cancelled all scheduled programmes for 72 hours
and switched to continuing live coverage.

> What we saw for three days running was a recycling of the horrors
> visually and as recounted by victims and witnesses; the aggressive,
> sometimes whiny, interviewing of officials who were reprimanded for
> the catastrophe, called to admit to the failure of their policies and/or
> resign; the reporters standing vigil at the decision-makers' doorstep to
> get word and or speculate on 'the most radical' solution, presumably
> cooking inside. And, in between we listened to the studio inmates
> selected for their talent of constantly inflating the drama. (ibid., p. 71)

This description seems all too familiar. The day-long coverage on the
Sunday of Diana's death saw the replaying of the details of the accident; the search for eyewitnesses; the juxtaposition of film and video
of Diana with violent images of the wrecked car; vox pop with
anguished and grieving members of the public; the accusations
hurled at the print media for causing her death; blame pointed at the
royal family for giving her a miserable life; quotes from politicians;
journalists standing outside the royal family's summer residence in
Balmoral in Scotland, waiting for any official or personal appearance; and endless studio speculation about the causes and
implications of the accident, and about the future of the royal family and the press. What makes the Israeli coverage different to that
of the Diana coverage is that, in Israel, the series of bombings constituted a direct and continuing threat to the safety and wellbeing of

members of Israeli society. Nonetheless, the immediate practical consequences of live 'marathonic' coverage were the same for the television coverage of the aftermath of Diana's death as for the Israeli bus bombings.

Live news operations require 'news' and 'live' information. Many respondents turned to television exactly because they wanted up-to-the-minute information. During such 'disaster marathons', however, live coverage means that there is a need to put news on air quickly and the urgency of the situation leaves little time for the usual journalistic procedures of fact-checking and verification (Liebes, 1998). After the princess's death, we saw in the section above that people were hungry for information, even if this later turned out to be inaccurate, and we can hypothesise that this is because such rumours allow room for discussion and speculation, and permit people to talk through the event and come to terms with it. There were, however, those respondents who were unhappy with the way that television was quick to report rumour as fact because this led to a wave of attacks on the paparazzi and the tabloid press:

I got the impression that some of the interviewers were looking for someone to blame for the accident – e.g. the paparazzi – even before the facts of what had happened had been established. (M71)

I was unhappy about television's instant reaction to fuel criticism of the paparazzi involved at the scene of the accident. It smacked of trial by television. (M22)

The need to find a rational cause for any accident or disaster is a common feature of television news. Yet the problem with disaster marathons is that they can lead to an emotionally charged reaction (Liebes, 1998). Interestingly, in the case of the death of Diana, there was certainly a tension between television news – which, due to the timing of the accident, was able to make a head start – and the print media. Thus, the emphasis on the role of the paparazzi became a major part of the news agenda that day and, according to Geraghty, had two functions. 'It allowed the television journalists to distance themselves from the excesses of the popular press, and also produced a "serious" issue for debate – the right to privacy.' (1998, p. 72). Some respondents saw this criticism of the press by broadcasters as hypocritical:

> There is something to be said for reporting events as they actually occur and knowing they may not have been edited. However it smacked of hypocrisy to criticise the paparazzi while showing shots, as close as they could manage, of the mangled wreckage in which the princess died. (F60)

As another respondent noted:

> The thing that galled me the most about the coverage was the hypocrisy of it all. One minute the media are being blamed for her death by harassing her, the next they've got their cameras in the Prime Minister's face asking stupid questions. (M22)

As well as the need to provide new and fresh stories, a related consequence of going to live extended coverage is the need to fill air time (Liebes, 1998). In the case of Diana, this was partly achieved by bringing on people who had met her or had worked with her on her many charitable projects. In many cases, these were important politicians – for example, Tony Blair, William Hague, Paddy Ashdown and foreign statesmen such as Bill Clinton and Nelson Mandela. At the same time, even in the morning, they were wheeling out 'rent-a-quote' MPs, such as David Mellor and Jeffrey Archer – who had themselves had their dirty laundry aired in the tabloid press and who were perhaps well qualified (and perhaps well motivated) to fuel criticism of the print media. Yet, as the day wore on, senior politicians increasingly gave way to persons working in charities, celebrities and television and pop stars.

> They seemed to wheel in every spare politician and media person they could to fill in the time and it ended up just inventing news. (F43)

This was such an unexpected event that everyone must have been
playing it by ear, so to speak. But a great deal was repetition, and some
of the interviews left much to be desired (e.g. Barbara Cartland).[3] I felt
that air time had to be filled – 'Who can we contact?' (F81)

The need to fill air time was also addressed by giving voice to a public response. As Schramm describes in his discussion of the US
coverage in the aftermath of the assassination of J. F. Kennedy, the
networks resorted to using interviews with members of the public
while they hastily assembled documentaries and tribute programmes
(1965). Yet the coverage devoted to the public response in vox pops
was not just as a result of filling in air time, but also a matter of filling in *space*. As Doane (1990) asserts in her examination of
'catastrophe television', television is usually not present when disaster strikes. As a result, television visits the scene in the aftermath to
give it a visual centre; it creates a space of catastrophe to make up
for the temporal lag. The location of the fateful car accident in an
underpass in Paris, however, created problems for the news coverage and may have had profound implications for the public response
which followed. The BBC correspondent Kate Adie, who covered
the news story from the scene of the accident, highlighted this very
issue the following year at the Edinburgh International Television
Festival.

Expressing surprise at the traffic travelling down the tunnel which
had quickly been reopened by the French authorities, Adie claimed,
'The cameraman and I looked at it and we both shook our heads,
because we knew we had a television problem. Anything we did was
going to look like a traffic report for *South East News.*' As a result,
Adie suggested that news images that day refocused on the solemn
crowds and beautiful flowers outside London palaces because it was
'something else to look at … not that concrete, smelly, traffic-ridden
underpass.'[4]

At the same time, the use of memorials and tributes from important people or members of the public is a well-worn journalistic
practice. The British journalist Mark Lawson has described this kind

of coverage as 'memorial broadcasting', where convention, as in ordinary life, dictates that the media cannot 'speak ill' of the recently deceased.[5] Such tributes are common when an important figure dies, but, as Lawson suggests, can often paint a distorted and romantic picture of the dead person. This may have had a particularly disorientating effect in the case of Diana's death because only a week previously, the print press had been critical of the princess. This becomes even more distorted when journalistic impartiality and distance become inflected with personal emotions; many of the respondents commented on how much the news presenters themselves seemed to be visibly upset by the news. As one respondent (F31) suggested, 'Right from the start there seemed to be a feeling of "We're all in it together."' While some respondents found these aspects of the television coverage comforting, it is inevitable that a potent combination of tributes, the pictures of crowds and the romantic portrayals of Diana's life would have compounded any sense of tragedy and unfairness.

In this sense, the need to fill air time with grieving associates and members of the public while providing comfort and reassurance to some members of the television audience also heightened the emotional charge of television that day. When television was able to compile filmed tributes and montages, these were startlingly moving. As Jenny Kitzinger pointed out in a *Screen* special debate, 'Television imagery was able to portray the living princess in very particular ways, starkly framing her death and constructing a seamless unity of grief', (Kitzinger, 1998, p. 76). Some respondents found such imagery or tributes either distasteful or upsetting.

What was bad was … the hastily broadcast 'Diana life stories' featuring montages of her appearances were quite sickly [sic]. (M20)

I think that the coverage was good as they kept us up to date with the events as well as looking back at Diana's life, although sometimes the latter made me more depressed. (F25)

The prominence of the coverage heightened my sense of loss. (F16)

From this we can certainly conclude that the television coverage that Sunday was not just extraordinary and extensive, but it was also dramatic and *emotive*. As Kitzinger argues, the 'dramatic juxtaposition' of the news of Diana's death with memorial footage of her life would have raised the 'emotional tempo' of the television coverage. 'Bulletin after bulletin showed images of the princess and then cut to pictures of the mangled wreckage of the car.' (1998, p. 77). Furthermore, while the coverage of Diana's death corresponds in most respects to 'disaster marathon' coverage, it was in one important respect very different. Diana, so popular wisdom had it, was 'the most photographed woman in the world'. That people followed her life and felt they knew her was an important factor in why some people felt so upset when she died. What was undoubtedly significant for the television coverage was that the miles of film and video footage of her when she was alive came into play in the obituaries and inserts on the day of the accident. This made her death harder to bear because she was *still* on television. As Williamson (1998) and Kitzinger (1998) have independently pointed out, for someone who had been so ever present in the media, the possibility that she could no longer exist seemed too much of a contradiction. 'Even as the television brought us endless further developments about her death, it also brought us endless further pictures.' (Williamson, 1998, p. 25). Herein lies the paradox, and a possible key as to why Diana's death may have proved so distressing, so impossible and *unthinkable*. On the one hand, television's authority, its combined use of words, images and charismatic personalities – all verified the truth that Diana was dead. Yet on the other, 'live' television found Diana's death hard to convey because, by constantly repeating memorial footage, it 'presented her as vibrantly alive' (Kitzinger, 1998, p. 76). This is perhaps why, in many respects, many viewers found it hard to come to terms with her death. As one respondent (F24) described: 'It didn't seem real. If Martyn Lewis turned around and said it was a mistake I think I would have accepted it easier and said "Oh, thank goodness for that," but no it was true!'

What made all these aspects of the broadcast output on the day the princess died so potent was again this need to fill air time during the marathon live coverage, the fact that interviews, clips, montages and breaking stories were constantly repeated and emphasised. While the day-long coverage permitted extended speculation and tributes, pictures of the princess and 'dramatic juxtapositions', the need to fill television output and the lack of real developments and new information meant that there was a substantial amount of repetition of reports and images. As Liebes argues in her discussion of 'disaster marathons', the repetition of the most poignant imagery and the 'juiciest lines' has the potential to impress itself more firmly on the viewer. 'As in music, sculpture or architecture, repetition carries a dynamic of its own, intensifying the images and the sounds while decontextualising them' (Liebes, 1998, p. 78). As a result, analytic discourse becomes even more confused with emotional responses, and any sense of loss, tragedy and confusion felt by the viewer will be rammed home in an almost Pavlovian viewing experience. As a result, the extraordinary, extensive and emotive coverage was also *emphatic*.

Following the Coverage and Emotional Exhaustion

So far we have seen that, for some people, the live television coverage brought some comfort to them in their distress; others recorded having their feelings heightened by the coverage or were dissatisfied that television was dedicated to this event all day. Yet *did* people watch it? First, it should be noted that 20 per cent of respondents did not watch *any* of the television coverage. This includes a number of respondents who were on holiday abroad, at work or occupied with prior engagements, irrespective of their response to the princess's death. Nonetheless, the fact that the accident occurred in the early hours of a Sunday morning meant that *potentially* many more people could have watched the coverage if they wanted to, in comparison to those able to watch it on a weekday. As it turns out, nearly a third of respondents did watch the coverage non-stop all day, hanging off every word, awaiting every update and seeking solace from their televisions:

> *We spent the whole day in the living room watching the news from 9.20 a.m. till 10.30 p.m.. No one got dressed and everyone cried – even my Dad.* (F16)

> *… we sat and watched – and watched – and watched, sometimes flicking from channel to channel, but never thinking of switching off, even though we were aware of the constant repetitions. Not eating – but making tea and drinking it, automatically until the stations themselves called halt and went off the air, at which point I observed (to wife), 'What a way to spend a day.'* (M75)

Nearly half of the respondents followed the coverage with interest throughout the day, fitting in their viewing with other activities or routines carried out at the weekend. Those who had to go out, either for prior engagements or to carry out necessary tasks such as shopping, recorded, for perhaps different reasons, a very strange atmosphere in the 'outside world':

> *The enormity probably took some time to sink in. Tried to dispel it by carrying on as normal, cycling, playing tennis with my friend as I do every Sunday morning. But there was an eerie feeling as I pedalled down the quiet roads – quieter than normal – wondering if the news was having the same effect on others behind closed doors.* (F44)

> *We had to go out for groceries, which I didn't feel like. When we got to the supermarket, I couldn't believe so many people were going about their usual business and that the Sunday papers had no mention of the deaths. We got back after 2 p.m., and watched as much ITN as we could handle.* (F27)

This last remark about watching 'as much ITN as we could handle' was common to a number of respondents who found the coverage emotionally exhausting and had to seek distraction from elsewhere. As the previous respondent went on to note, 'The day's events weighed so heavy by 8 p.m. we craved escapism.' Another respondent (F55) remarked: 'I stuck with the BBC all afternoon, but watched ITV in the evening, as there is a limit to how much emotion you can take, although I was weepy for over a week.'

Interestingly, a look at the television ratings[6] in the early evening on that Sunday also perhaps reveals that there was a limit to how much of the extensive coverage people could watch – because either their emotions or interest had been exhausted. While BBC 1 continued to show tribute and news programmes on the Sunday evening, ITV broke the marathon coverage at 7.30 p.m. to broadcast the scheduled edition of *Coronation Street*, followed by the popular drama *Heartbeat* at 8.00 p.m. What is interesting is that both of these programmes pulled in audiences of more than 13.5 million each, compared to the tribute programmes on BBC 1, which attracted audiences of between 4 and 4.5 million. These ITV programmes, and other programmes in the same ITV scheduling slot, regularly attract high ratings, but these figures were higher than usual. The previous year on the same Sunday (1 September 1996), popular drama and light entertainment on ITV at the same time (*Heartbeat, You've Been Framed, London's Burning*) had attracted audiences of between 10 and 11.5 million. This compared to BBC 1 audiences of more than 7 million and nearly 9 million, respectively, for a popular factual programme and a major Hollywood film (*Robin Hood, Prince of Thieves*, Kevin Reynolds, 1991). What the higher figures for popular drama on ITV on the day the princess died suggest is that some people *did* want to see other programmes or experience some relief from the emotional onslaught of the Diana coverage.

Summary

In this chapter we have seen that many respondents were deeply shocked and distressed on learning the news about the Princess of Wales's death. That the news spread to households throughout that Sunday morning through radio and word of mouth indicates that people were not initially watching television. Yet, when the news broke, where possible (and where interested), many of the BFI's respondents turned to television for more information, either seeking the verification of television images over the sounds of radio, or being unable to believe what their friends or family members were telling them.

When people turned to television, what they found was *extraordinary* in that it was relaying information about an extraordinary news event, while at the same time extraordinarily disrupting all the mainstream terrestrial schedules. The coverage was also *extensive* in that it ran for long periods on the three main channels, indeed running all day on BBC 1. It was *emotive*, through dramatic juxtapositions, upset and empathetic newsreaders, and almost soft-focus tribute programmes which heightened any sense of tragedy. Finally, the coverage was *emphatic* in that the need to fill air time and the lack of new information meant that stories and images were recycled and repeated, further heightening any emotional reactions. While some respondents found elements of the television coverage reassuring because it provided information and showed how other people felt, others were irritated by what they felt to be excessive, hypocritical and sentimental coverage.

Notes

1. While 40 per cent of respondents specifically claimed to be shocked or shattered on hearing the news, 11 per cent claimed to be sombre, sad or depressed.
2. Geoff Ellis, 'The news that shook the world', *Radio Times*, 13–19 September 1997, p. 27.
3. The romance novelist Barbara Cartland was actually Diana's step-grandmother.
4. Janine Gibson, 'TV news "has heart" since Diana's death', *The Guardian*, 31 August 1998, p. 6.
5. Mark Lawson, 'Sky and CNN were first, but a royal death is a BBC matter', *The Guardian*, 1 September 1997, p. 7.
6. Source: Broadcasters' Audience Research Board (BARB) Ltd.

2
The Grieving Audience?

In the aftermath of the Princess of Wales's death, one of the major focuses of television attention was the display and outpouring of 'public grief'. On the day that the princess died, the prime minister Tony Blair stated that he was 'utterly devastated' and that Britain was 'a nation in state of shock, in mourning, in grief that is so deeply painful for us'.[1] This 'grief' appeared to be verified on the day of the accident by television images of shaken newsreaders, expressions of sorrow and tributes from the great and the good, opinion and comment from around the country, and the first pictures of people arriving outside London palaces with flowers and messages. In an attempt to understand this 'public' reaction, the BFI asked respondents whether the death of the princess had had an 'impact' on them 'personally'. Fifty per cent of respondents stated that it *did* affect them personally. Many of these wrote of how shocked they were, of how much they cried, of how – echoing the words of the prime minister – they, too, were 'devastated'. In one instance, a respondent (F68) wrote, 'I feel as if I had suffered a death in the family.' Many wrote of how they were surprised at their own feelings:

> As many other people have said, Diana's death upset me far more than I would have expected. I was surprised how shocked, and later depressed, I was by the accident. Several weeks later I am still finding it difficult to believe what has happened. (M49)

What follows here concerns the responses of that half of the BFI sample which claimed to be personally affected. The 50 per cent of respondents who denied that the princess's death had an impact on them has implications for the way we should think about the 'public' response to the princess's death and the apparent 'unity in grief' depicted in the media. This will be explored in the next chapter.

Good Grief?

Whether the emotional reaction of Tracking Study respondents to the princess's death constitutes grief is difficult to assess. As we saw in the previous chapter, 40 per cent of Tracking Study respondents expressed feelings of shock, disbelief and distress on hearing the news of the princess's death, with some spontaneously bursting into tears. This prefigured any exposure to the subsequent extended media coverage. This is consistent with reactions to the news of the Kennedy assassination in 1963, reactions which were taken by Sheatsley and Feldman (1965) to signify the initial stages of grief. However, the assassination of a democratically elected head of state has particular symbolic and practical implications. This was especially the case with Kennedy, a relatively young, charismatic leader who had led a country on the brink of nuclear war in 1962. Thus the responses recorded by Sheatsley and Feldman (1965), Schramm (1965) and Mindak and Hursch (1965) may equally be related to a disruption of normality, or a sense of threat to both national and personal security.

The problem here is that it is difficult to verify or qualify the depth of reaction experienced by the different BFI respondents. There is no objective measurement. The best that can be hoped for here is that respondents' self-reporting of distress or upset would have been measured against their everyday emotional condition and stability. As such, their responses should be taken seriously, but do not necessarily signal grief. Similarly, a separate psychological study conducted by Shevlin et al. (1999) three weeks after the princess's death recorded a measurable degree of psychological distress in a significant number of the people surveyed. The results of that study, too, remain unclear as to whether the psychological reaction was specifically grief (Walter, 1999b).

Nonetheless, Walter, a sociologist specialising in the study of death, bereavement and funeral culture, argues that the emotional response which followed the princess's death was 'real' grief (1999b). He qualifies this, however, by adding that it was short lived and that the Diana mourners 'were not left with an empty bed, with nobody to hold them, with one less at the dinner table or with nobody to bring in the bread' (1999b, p. 34). Yet where BFI respondents actually use the term 'grief', they appear to acknowledge that it may be different to other experiences of bereavement:

I found I was upset, emotional and depressed from her death until days after the funeral. I have never grieved like this before and I still cannot understand why it had such an impact on me. (F40)

I lost my own father last November, which was a terrible shock. I grieve for him still. My grief for Diana is different, I can't describe it. (F39)

The respondents who replied that they had been personally affected were encouraged to explain their feelings. Some respondents in this half of the sample, like the two quoted above, were unable to account for their feelings. Of the rest, their responses can be grouped together in six broad categories. These were:

- The princess's death triggered memories of a prior bereavement.
- It was shocking that someone who had been ever present in the media should die so suddenly.
- Respondents had identified with the Princess of Wales or her experiences in some way, or had admired her personal qualities.
- It made them think about the two princes left behind or about how their own families might cope in such circumstances.
- It made them think about their own mortality.
- It was a tragic event.

Many of these BFI respondents identified more than one of the above thoughts or emotional reactions. Of course, emotional responses to events or situations are extremely complex and some of the reasons that some people felt so affected may have involved processes so taken for granted as to be unremarkable or unconscious. It is also likely that multiple, overlapping and perhaps even contradictory processes were at work in different people. As a result, it is simply not possible to account fully for why the princess's death provoked such an emotional response.

What is common to each of the experiences described above, with very few exceptions and in common with most of the UK public, is the fact that Tracking Study respondents had never come into contact with or met the Princess of Wales.[2] This raises a fundamental but ultimately tricky question. How is it possible to grieve over someone that you have never met? There are two possible responses to this. The first is that people experienced grief because the princess played a part in their lives in some way. The second is that people's responses to the princess's death were not specifically grief, but another kind of emotional or psychological response. The answer probably lies somewhere between these two positions.

Yet for most people their only experience of the Princess of Wales would have been mediated. This suggests that media processes and constructions were crucial to how the princess was perceived in both life and death. It is therefore the modest aim of the rest of this chapter to explore two aspects of the emotional responses to the princess's death. The first aspect relates to respondents' previous experience of bereavement. This is discussed briefly here because it was raised by several respondents and because it has been referred to in other literature (for example, Walter, 1999b). It is an area that also has some psychological validity. The second aspect concerns the way in which television narratives are constitutive of processes by which people understand the everyday world. This will receive a far more extended discussion.

Prior Bereavement

The death of the Princess of Wales caused distress among some members of the television audience by reactivating loss associated with prior bereavement. The postponement of feelings of grief and distress at the time of death is a common response to bereavement (Lindemann, 1965). This postponement may last for several years and any number of causes can precipitate a delayed reaction. It has previously been proposed that Diana's death may have caused such a reaction (Cathcart, 1997; Walter, 1999b) and the responses of several Tracking Study respondents suggest that this was the case for some people:

> ... weeping watching TV but that is because I 'relived' a major bereavement (and the grief reaction is still there). (F46)

> It was also the saddest event for me in some time – before that John Smith – and before that my father's death (by suicide) in 1971. But, like others whose close relatives died, I was unable to cry tears for him. I am not sure why people cry more for someone they have never met; perhaps TV does stir up the emotions. (F56)

A common reaction to death is a feeling of guilt. 'The bereaved searches the time before the death for evidence of failure to do right by the loved one' (Lindemann, 1965, p. 188). Yet if some people were reliving prior bereavement following the death of the Princess of Wales, the reactivation of feelings of grief may also have triggered or renewed feelings of guilt which were then complicated for feelings for Diana, as the following respondent suggests:

> I was surprisingly very low all week and it was on my mind most of the time. I wasn't a huge Diana fan but I did admire her for what she did for others, but felt more depressed about her than when my grandparents died – I loved them and that made me feel very guilty. (F32)

Furthermore, previous bereavement was not the only painful event of which people were reminded. As the following respondent demonstrates, people bring with them their own experiences of life when watching events depicted on television:

> *I was involved in an horrific RTA [road traffic accident] in 1994. I have disabilities, both mental and physical. My children were with me. We survived, but there were times when I wish we had not. I grieved for my lost life. Grieved for the lost life of my children. It was all a dreadful emotional and physical mess. We have come through it, and I live a very happy and fulfilled life. When the news broke, I relived my own and my children's ordeal. (F45)*

Nonetheless, that Diana's death triggered memories of painful experiences or bereavement raises further questions which return us to the larger subject here of the media constitution of everyday life. If delayed grief can be triggered by any number of causes, why did the death of Diana have this effect in particular as opposed to the reporting or depiction of any other death in the media? News programmes often contain details about fatal road accidents or major disasters, and television dramas often involve plot lines about death (for example, hospital dramas grounded in realism such as *Casualty* on BBC 1).[3] Furthermore, why did this particular event affect so many people at the same time? The answer to these questions perhaps lies in the way the media, and television in particular, helps construct our view of everyday life and this will be explored in the next section.

Ontological Security and Symbolic Resources

Television contributes daily to our knowledge of the world and our place within it. It contributes to what Giddens describes as *ontological security*, a confidence which exists at an emotional rather than cognitive level, and one which people have in themselves and the world around them. Trust is a precondition of ontological security – in people, systems, institutions and events. In a changing, risk-filled world, this trust is sustained 'through the ordered communities of language, routine, habit, the taken for granted ... the familiar and the predictable' (Silverstone: 1994, pp. 18–19). Thus the 'dailiness' of television means that watching confirms, affirms, reaffirms and reinforces that life still goes on as normal, business as usual, that this is 'the way things are'. It does this through its punctuation of and interaction with the everyday lives of its viewers, and through its content. 'Television is very much part of the taken for granted seriality and spatiality of everyday life.' (Silverstone, 1994, p. 19). What this means is that the continuing nature of television corresponds to the continuing routine, habitual and repetitive nature of everyday life; this is tied to temporal and spatial structures of when, where and how people watch television and with whom. At the same time, television content also contributes towards ontological security by representing and reflecting aspects of daily life that are familiar to viewers. While a news programme, for example, may focus on a geographical location that the viewer has never visited, and is perhaps never likely to visit, the televisual text contributes to ontological security at a fundamental level by reflecting and repeating pre-existing knowledge and expectations (and prejudice) about that location. The repetition of this knowledge and language on a daily basis inscribes and re-inscribes the relationship between television and the lived world.

This relationship is also crucial in individual identity formation. Individuals have to fashion for themselves a sense of identity using a variety of resources from around them. At the same time, however, the changing and risk-filled nature of the world implies that identity formation is a never ending and reflexive enterprise (Giddens, 1990; 1991). As a result, the routines and habitual practices that help constitute ontological security are essential for negotiating a continuous sense of self. As social and interpersonal relations have become increasingly fragmented and subject to change in the 'modern' world, and as media consumption has become an increasingly perpetual condition of society, the nature of identity formation has had to change. Increasingly, individuals have resorted to 'mediated experience' for symbolic resources to 'inform and refashion' their identities (Thompson, 1995, p. 233). Thus individuals use the media, as well as material culture, as tools and resources, as a form of *bricolage*, to construct their own identities. This is not just simply a matter of conscious imitation of a fashionable film or rock star, for example. These symbolic resources include know-how, vicarious experience, social and cultural competencies, identifications and recognitions. Like Lévi-Strauss–ian myths, they are 'good to think with' (1966).

One way that individuals can make sense of their experience and identity is through the 'storying of the self'. This is because '[s]tructuring experience in narrative terms creates order out of chaos and gives meaning to what otherwise would be experienced as anarchic or fragmented' (Finnegan, 1997, p. 76). Yet, while narratives constitute one of the strategies which people deploy to understand and make sense of their lives, this is culturally dependent. 'Given their constructed nature and dependence upon the cultural conventions and language usage, life narratives obviously reflect the prevailing theories about "possible lives" that are part of one's culture' (Bruner, 1987, p. 15). In this sense, the stories that the individual uses to conceptualise the self can conceivably come from all kinds of available media genres. What is worth exploring, therefore, is the extent to which the Princess of Wales's life story can be perceived to adhere to the generic conventions of some media narratives. Comparing Tracking Study responses, it will then be possible to speculate about the extent to which these narratives informed ways in which members of the television audience thought about themselves.

Diana, Soap and Melodramatic Identifications

There have been numerous comparisons between the royal family, Diana's life and the television soap opera format (Aron and Livingstone, 1997; Geraghty, 1998; Street, 1997; Wilson, 1998). According to Geraghty (1998), for example, there were four ways in which Diana's life 'story' could be understood and that the public's responses deployed or rejected these narratives 'in an ambivalent and complex way' (1998, p. 70). These narratives were the fairy tale, the 'classic narrative' (marked by disruption and restoration of stability), the soap opera narrative and the news story. Until the princess's death, Geraghty suggests that the soap opera form of narrative was the most attractive way of understanding her life because, unlike the fairy tale and 'classic' forms, soap operas lack formal closure and have a never-ending quality. As we will see, this never-ending quality also has much in common with the seriality of news. Indeed, Ellis has argued that the only difference between television soap opera and the news is the actual source material (1982). As we will explore later, what transforms the Diana story is that her death becomes a *particular* kind of news narrative.

Apart from continuous story lines, there are a number of other reasons why the television soap opera narrative is compelling here. In the first instance, a common element of soap opera is that there is always a set of interweaving stories and a cluster of characters (Geraghty, 1981; Livingstone, 1998; Allen, 1995). These are sometimes set around a family (Jordan, 1981). It is in this way that '[w]e have long grown used to the idea that the whole of the Royal Family has become a soap opera' (Wilson, 1998, p. 117). Secondly, Jordan states that an important element in the soap opera narrative is the quest for a partner in life (1981). The 'Royal Wedding', the divorce, the affairs, and finally the princess's ill-fated liaison with Dodi Al Fayed certainly seemed to revolve around the finding, loss and re-finding of a partner. Thirdly, as others have noted, for example Jordan in connection with *Coronation Street* (1981), television soap operas have substantial roles for women and allow room for strong characters. Yet, as Geraghty goes on to argue, 'Most crucially though, as feminist critics have shown, it [soap opera] reversed traditional values by privileging the feminine world in which emotion, empathy and talk were the means by which life could best be understood and managed' (1998). Crucially, Diana may be perceived as a strong female character who championed that world of emotion and empathy.

The soap opera narrative also has particular appeal here because it allows 'for villainesses as well as heroines' and for protagonists 'to change positions and attributes along with the twists and turns of the plot' (Geraghty, 1998, p. 71). As in soap opera, Diana's 'character' had to endure the ignominy of problems, conflicts, affairs and divorces, and change positions, attitudes and guises along the way. These guises included the fairy-tale princess, the 'touchy-feely' mother, the wronged and vengeful woman, the promiscuous woman, the political meddler and finally the 'People's Princess'. In this respect, Diana constituted an ideal soap opera heroine.

It is the different subject positions that Diana occupied within the royal soap opera and the life situations that she experienced that perhaps made it easier for a range of people, especially women, to identify with her. It was such women, predominantly in their thirties, forties and fifties, who wrote some of the most articulate and self-aware replies:

I did not have a happy childhood myself and, like her, I have sometimes felt out of control in the past as I've worked my way through various traumas to reach the point I'm at now. I think I would have found the growth I've achieved very difficult to arrive at had I been in the public eye with millions of people clearly expecting something from me. I feel a certain respect for Princess Diana that she managed to hang on with gritted teeth almost and deliver a substantial amount of good despite her own difficulties. (F36)

I was devastated. She was a very special member of the Royal Family and reminded me so much of myself. I too had a loveless marriage – I felt so deeply sad inside but never showed it to others. I tried to be happy, I too suffered an eating disorder because I was so dreadfully unhappy. Deep down I was crying out for help but no one understood. My husband said I was seeking attention and had no sympathy. (F46)

As this respondent went on to add: 'I have a new partner now and I am extremely happy. I believe Diana was too when she died. So many times had I thought of suicide – no one would miss me. Thankfully she and I overcame these feelings and found happiness.'

It should still be remembered, however, that people only apprehended Diana's life through the media, and media constructions conform to various generic and narrative conventions. In this sense, the way that Diana was represented has much in common with what Ang describes as the 'melodramatic heroine' (1996). This is worth extended discussion here because it demonstrates the emotional potency of recognition and identification while showing, at the same time, how such identifications are intricately interwoven with how people perceive the world and reflexively imagine and fashion their own identities.

In her study of the US soap *Dallas*, Ang (1985) sought to discover why people enjoyed watching the ups and downs of a fictional family set in the rich and glamorous world of Texas oil barons. While the plot's dramatic twists and turns were overdetermined and melodramatic, and while the level of wealth, the wheeling and dealing, and the politicking of this family were well beyond the bounds and experiences of the typical viewer, Ang discovered that a lot of people liked it because they found something realistic in it. Ang argued that, for viewers to become 'involved' in *Dallas*, they had to experience both the characters and the fictional world as 'real'. Viewers experienced this at a connotative level – the associated meanings of the fiction – rather than a denotative level – the literal and manifest content. In particular, what viewers found realistic at a connotative level were the veracity of the family disputes and the emotional and psychological turmoil of some of the characters. Ang calls this 'emotional realism'.

What is significant here, and this is interesting in light of Giddens's discussion of the emotional nature of ontological security, is that the experience of *Dallas* has no relationship with cognitive processes, but is entirely emotional. 'What is recognised as real is not knowledge of the world, but a subjective experience of the world: a "structure of feeling"' (Ang, 1985, p. 45).[4] In this 'structure of feeling', emotions are always being stirred up:

> ... life is characterised by an endless fluctuation between happiness and
> unhappiness, that life is a question of falling down and getting up

again. This structure of feeling can be called the tragic structure of feeling; tragic because of the idea that happiness can never last forever but, quite the contrary, is precarious. (ibid., p. 46)

It is the recognition of this, Ang argues, which causes pleasure for the viewer. Nonetheless, this 'tragic structure of feeling' is not recognised by everyone, but only by people who possess a 'melodramatic imagination' (ibid.).

It is this 'melodramatic imagination' and the recognition of a 'tragic structure of feeling' which allow many viewers to identify with the character Sue Ellen, in particular. Sue Ellen is married to one of the central protagonists, J. R. Ewing – she is an alcoholic, is constantly 'on a war footing' with her husband and is in a 'constant state of crisis' (1985, p. 7). Although Sue Ellen's material existence may be vastly different from most viewers, the experiences and difficulties she faces have an emotional resonance with those viewers. Her alcoholism, for example, serves as a cipher for her psychological condition. Yet, despite Sue Ellen's attempts to flee her miserable existence, the viewer knows that she is ultimately powerless and unable to avoid the torments devised by the script. It is particularly women who identify with this position, argues Ang, because it is women who tend to feel trapped and powerless within society. As a result, Ang states:

The melodramatic imagination should be regarded as a psychological strategy to overcome the material meaninglessness of everyday existence, in which routine and habit prevail in human relationships as much as elsewhere. (1985, p. 79)

By making mundane and ordinary experience special and meaningful, this sense of 'material meaninglessness' can be dissipated or mitigated in some way. In her later work, Ang develops this position to describe Sue Ellen as a 'melodramatic heroine'. While all characters are essentially polysemous, Ang argues that 'a basic agreement seems to exist that her [Sue Ellen's] situation is an extremely contentious and frustrating one, and her personality is rather tormented' (1996, pp. 87–8). Many women identify with Sue Ellen, therefore, because her 'subject position is characterised by a sense of entrapment ...' (ibid., p. 91).

Ang goes on to argue that in watching soap operas such as *Dallas*, pleasure can be derived from taking up subject positions beyond the constraints of everyday life and by exploring other lives and possibilities. With strong similarities to Giddens's reflexive project of the self, Ang states that being a woman involves constant *work* of self-reconstruction. For example, women's magazines show 'how to be a true woman', but women are expected to achieve such a state effortlessly (Ang, 1996). For Ang, the relationship between the melodramatic imagination and the project of self-(re)construction has two consequences. The first is the feeling that it is impossible to have everything under control at the same time. In a Marx-ian formulation, life is always lived under circumstances not of one's own making. Secondly, 'identification with a melodramatic character like Sue Ellen also validates those feelings by offering women some room to indulge in them, to let go as it were, in a moment of intense, self-centred abandon, a moment of giving up to the social circumstances, just like Sue Ellen has done, so that the work of the self-(re)construction is no longer needed' (Ang, 1996, p. 95). Ang concludes that 'such moments, however, fleeting, can be experienced as moments in which the complexity of the task of being a woman is fully realised and accepted', and as a result it is '[n]o wonder melodrama is accompanied by tears.'

It would appear that such discussion is highly relevant for considering audience responses to the death of the Princess of Wales for the very reason that she was constructed and/or perceived as a melodramatic heroine. Although Diana had an apparently glamorous and wealthy life, she 'suffered', and 'it was this suffering and its confessional quality that aligned her with the "ordinary", everyday, mundane struggles of living modern forms of existence' (Blackman, 1999, p. 111). She was popularly perceived to have been trapped between her royal duty and her self-fulfilment and care for her sons.

A cold and heartless royal family apparently cast her aside, while her husband indulged in an extramarital affair. Her eating disorder, like Sue Ellen's alcoholism, was an explicit hint at the emotional and psychological turmoil inside. Her attempts to escape and find love were exposed in the tabloid press. For those who perhaps possess a melodramatic imagination, there may have been an intense recognition of her powerlessness, her entrapment, and the ups and downs in her life.

Yet while the concept of the melodramatic imagination is a theoretical construct, the respondents quoted above who wrote of their difficult experiences seem to hint that life *is* full of ups and downs. As the 36-year-old female respondent went on to conclude: 'My first thought when I learned of the death was that she was about as lucky as me – I could see me finding some degree of happiness and being struck by sudden tragedy!' This hints at a sense of resignation, of fate, that life is a precarious mix of highs and lows, and perhaps evidence here of a melodramatic imagination at work, or in construction.

Public Knowledge and Shared History

At the same time, Diana's repeated exposure in the media may have had two further consequences of significance here. First, the details and events of Diana's life seemed to be open to public scrutiny through the media. Such details, as discussed, may provide a symbolic resource for identity formation and (re-)creation as suggested by Thompson (1995). It is perhaps this which helped foster a sense of shared subjective experience for those with something like a melodramatic imagination. Secondly, the appearance of the princess in the media over a period of sixteen years may have perpetuated a sense of co-temporality, as an age cohort, and contributed to the never-ending quality which news shares with television soap opera. Both these points are important because, unlike in other news stories about accidents or disaster, people had prior knowledge of the princess – they may have felt that they knew her in some way and that they had known her for a long time.

Thompson has argued that today's media allows new forms of intimacy to develop (1995). In what he describes as quasi-mediated interaction, the individual can establish a social relationship with distant others through the media. This relationship can be characterised by bonds of friendship, affection or loyalty; however, because this is monologic, information flows only one way – these bonds are non-reciprocal:

> In the case of mediated quasi-interaction, individuals can create and establish a form of intimacy which is essentially non-reciprocal. It is this new form of mediated, non-reciprocal intimacy stretched across time and space, which underlies, for example, the relationship between fan and star. It can be exhilarating, precisely because it is freed from the reciprocal obligations characteristic of face-to-face interaction. (Thompson, 1995, p. 208)

In other words, it is possible to have a relationship with someone on the television screen without actually expending any effort or commitment. It is this which encourages the feeling which can be summed up by the phrase: 'If we met, I bet we would be friends.'

Most individuals sustain this kind of relationship with actors, actresses, rock and pop stars, newsreaders and celebrities to some extent. Gauntlett and Hill found that many Tracking Study respondents regarded newsreaders and presenters as trusted and valued friends (1999). It is in exactly this way, therefore, that Diana's repeated exposure in the media may have provided a 'regular and dependable' range of subject positions with which people could identify or, in Ang's sense, give themselves up to. There can, however, be negative consequences of this. These are what Thompson describes as 'the double-bind of mediated dependency'. He describes this as: 'The more the process of self-formation is enriched by mediated symbolic forms, the more the self becomes dependent on media systems which lie beyond its control' (1995, p. 214). Such relationships may on some occasions become the source of anguish or pain. This can occur when fans become aware of the physical segregation between the site of media production and site of media consumption

(Couldry, 1999; Vermorel and Vermorel, 1985), which in turn denies them direct access to the focus of their attention.

Diana had been a known face in the media for a relatively long time. Indeed, one of the reasons cited by respondents for feeling upset was the sense that she had been ever present in the media and that once she died her absence was hard to comprehend, as the following two respondents note:

> *It would have been tragic whoever it happened to, but it acquired a personal dimension because we knew so much about this woman and had seen so much of her that it was as if we knew her personally. Almost.* (F37)

> *It seems strange, writing this three weeks on from the event, but her death still seems almost unreal. I remember during the week itself, every now and again stopping myself when I realised she was gone. She had seemed so much part of our lives for almost 20 years, every magazine, newspaper, TV station covered her every move extensively, that without knowing her, even less approving of what she stood for, I have to admit feeling quite a profound sense of loss.* (M45)

Whether or not people followed Diana's life closely, it was hard not to be aware of her or her presence in the media. She was always around, never too far from the public spotlight. On television, the stories about the Princess of Wales often featured in news programmes, which often responded to articles in the tabloid press or in magazines. As we have already suggested, with her appearance in the news on a frequent basis between 1981 and 1997, Diana was very much like a regular cast member in a television serial. It is this very seriality which news bulletins share with soap operas. There is no narrative closure; there is a 'continuous reconfiguration of events'; there is a perpetual return to the present, with a stable cast of characters and problems. As Allen has observed, serials are 'a form of narrative organised around institutionally imposed gaps in the text' (1995, p. 17). So, between each news item, or at least between each time that

Diana appeared in the news, life would have developed in the same way that individuals' lives develop and move on. This sense of shared continuous history strengthens any bonds of perceived intimacy with public personalities or television characters. In comparing the relationship between the 'movement of time' in the fictional world of soap opera and the 'real' world, for example, Scannell asserts:

> ... since these move in parallel and at the same pace, it follows that the lifetime of viewers and listeners unfolds at the same rate as the lives of the characters in the story. Thus, one stands in the same temporal relation to them as one does to one's own family, relatives, friends and everyday acquaintances. (1996, p.159)

In just the same way that they can catch up with friends or relatives after a period of time, viewers can drop in and out of long-running soap opera or news narratives. There is a sense of co-temporality – events take place at the same time, in real-life time. Characters and people on television are like age cohorts and people's lives keep time in step. As a result, the conjunction of identification with the princess and an awareness of a shared chronology may have had a powerful resonance with some people, as the following respondent suggests:

> *Yes I was upset. She and I were the same age (she was six months younger) so I had been interested in following her story from the start. At first I was envious, I suppose, of her, but as time went on I realised the impossible strains on her. There is no way I would have changed places with her. Now she will forever be 36, I'm 37 in November. As a mother, I realise what a tragic loss it will be for the 'boys'.* (F36)

Further still, the continuous nature of television soap opera and news means there is speculation on television itself, in other media and in the street, playground, factory or office about what the characters are going to do next or how events may develop and what the implications of their actions are. There is a sense of continuous time and a sense of future (Geraghty, 1981). There is no ending and there is no 'happy ever after'. Just as in Diana's life, just as in the lives of millions of people, major wedding set pieces are followed by marital discord and often divorce. It was in exactly the same way that rejoicing in the news over the fall of the Berlin Wall and the end of the Cold War was eventually followed by East–West tension over the Kosovo and Chechnya conflicts. Soap operas, history and daily life continues.

Victims, Mortality and Death's Irreversibility

When Diana died, the processes described above may have been thrown into confusion and chaos. In ordinary and daily news stories involving death – such as road accidents and murders at home, and wars, famines and natural disasters abroad – the victims are unknown to most people. Until that particular news bulletin, these victims did not effectively exist for the television audience. After their death and after the bulletin, these victims once again no longer exist. These victims only exist momentarily *in* death.

Yet Diana was different because, as we have seen, people had pre-existing knowledge about her. Through the identification with different subject positions, particularly through the prism of a melodramatic imagination, the sense of mediated intimacy with a distant other – and the continuous co-temporality of shared 'lifetime', many people felt they knew or understood the Princess of Wales.[5] As a result, even though most people had never met Diana, when she died it was as if they had lost someone they knew well, someone to which they had a connection.

As well as constituting an experience akin to some kind of bereavement, Diana's death also had other implications for how people see the world and themselves. Some may still have apprehended her death with the kind of melodramatic imagination we have referred to previously. Indeed, her new-found romance and happiness denied at the moment of its realisation in a dramatic but sordid road accident is the stuff of melodrama, and has much in common with television soap operas and even classic Hollywood tear-jerkers. Wilson argues, for example, that Diana's death had elements of 'operatic tragedy' which 'fits with a long western tradition of doomed love, of romantic passion as inextricably linked to death' (Wilson, 1998, p. 116). It was this element of tragedy and fate which may have prompted the following comments:

> *I'm glad this young woman appeared to have found personal happiness in the final days of her life before she was disillusioned, as she surely would have been before many years were over.* (F77)

In a sense, this is almost a recognition of the soap opera genre where happiness is only momentary – there are only temporary resolutions to personal, emotional and relationship problems. Yet this respondent goes to on to allude to that closure inherent in other forms of melodrama or tragedy: 'Perhaps it was destined that this should happen.' As other respondents noted:

> *Such a sudden, premature and ill-timed death would, in a work of fiction, be dismissed as too cruel and sad to be believed.* (M42)

> *Diana's death was a massive shock to me for its suddenness, but I was half expecting it. There was an inevitability about it which I find hard to explain.* (M48)

Although Diana's death may have belonged to a particular canon of celebrity death, and the melodramatic trajectory of her life may have pointed to such a sad conclusion, her death also showed up the world as a potentially brutal and arbitrary place. This is because Diana became a *victim*.

In Langer's definition of the 'victim' category of news story, individuals are 'caught up in circumstances of adversity beyond their immediate control' (Langer, 1998, pp. 76–7). In these situations, the news item will draw the viewer into a relationship not of spectatorship, but of involvement, because '[a] "good victim" is above all a person, "character" to whom one can relate' (1998, p. 80). As a consequence, 'Conditions which produce good victims must be understood to "approach disaster" shattering everyday experience socially and psychologically' (1998, p. 79). For the reasons discussed in this chapter, Diana was indeed a 'good victim'.

Psychologically, such news stories are shattering because they demonstrate that our very own survival may be at stake. Accidents will happen. Thus:

> The untimely death of a young person upsets our sense of fairness and if that death is sudden, it disrupts our sense of control and predictability over the world. A generation which has grown up with Diana will have confronted its own vulnerability. (Cathcart, 1997, pp. 503–4)

Ordinarily, with people living longer and death sequestrated into special institutions (Ariès, 1976; Bauman, 1992; Mellor, 1993), death is something that is not normally encountered among young or middle-aged people. With Diana, a known person of the same or a similar age has died. This is unusual – yet it could have been us. Indeed, many of those who said they were profoundly affected by the princess's death said that it made them think about their own mortality. This was demonstrated particularly by the two following young respondents:

> *It has shown me just how vulnerable people are and made me think more about death and that if it can happen to someone important like Diana with all her protection etc it can happen to any of us.* (F25)

> *It made me realise how vulnerable we all are. If such a beautiful, young, vivacious woman could die in such a tragic way, so suddenly, then surely this shows just how precious life is.* (M18)

At the same time, Diana's death may have been socially and psychologically shattering because the experience of death can upset a stable sense of ontological security. As we have seen, such security in the world, in Mellor's clear formulation of Giddens (1990, 1991):

... refers to persons having a sense of order and continuity in relation to the events in which they participate, and the experiences they have, in their day-to-day lives.... Ontological security therefore depends upon persons being able to find meaning in their lives. (Mellor, 1993, p. 12)

Yet death's irrationality and arbitrariness destabilises that order and continuity. Death is discontinuous. It not only threatens the way the world is perceived, but it also has implications for the way individuals perceive themselves. In the constant re-creation and re-negotiation of self-identity (not in circumstances of one's own making), identity is always subject to change. Or, following Ang, new subjective positions can be taken up whenever identifying with a new soap opera (or film) character. Whereas the melodramatic imagination is an attempt to create meaning out of the humdrum of everyday life, death calls into question that meaning (Mellor, 1993). It shatters ontological security; it calls everything into question:

Death is particularly disturbing because it signals a threatened 'irreality' of the self-projects which modernity encourages individuals to embark upon, an ultimate absence of meaning, the presence of death bringing home to them the existential isolation of the individual in high modernity. (Mellor, 1993, pp. 19–20)

As Bauman (1992) and Mellor (1993) both note, death proves the futility of the project of self-(re)construction. Death is *irreversible*. It is 'the absolute *other* of being, an *unimaginable* other' (Bauman, 1992, p. 2. Bauman's emphasis). There is no longer an identity which can again be renegotiated. In Bauman's words, 'Death means dissent into personalized nothingness ... Depersonalization is personal' (ibid., p. 51).

Summary
Fifty per cent of BFI respondents claimed to have been personally affected by the Princess of Wales's death, although it is hard to assess whether or not this constitutes grief. What is clear is that most

people had never met the princess; this means that previous knowledge and experience of her had been mediated. The media articulation of Diana's life in the news had an analogous relationship with soap opera narratives. On the one hand, this meant that people felt that they knew her and that they had known her for a long time. On the other hand, this also meant that there may have been some recognition of Diana as a 'melodramatic heroine', and a recognition of entrapment and powerlessness as a shared condition of womanhood.

Familiarity with such people, life stories and experiences, whether mediated or first hand, helps form the tools and resources for identity formation and self-construction, and for establishing trust and confidence in everyday life. In a world that is becoming increasingly mediated, people are perhaps becoming more dependent on media images, characters and depictions to provide the resources to help establish identities and trust. When someone in the media such as the Princess of Wales dies, these processes collapse. In a sense, therefore, the death of Diana both demonstrated the tragic fate of a melodramatic heroine struggling to gain control of her life and highlighted the futility and meaninglessness of such struggle. The princess's death provided evidence of our own vulnerability in the world, the futility of our petty struggles for happiness and the potential meaninglessness of existence.

Notes

1. Vivek Chaudhary, 'Devastated Blair leads tributes of "nation in shock"', *The Guardian*, 1 September 1997, p. 7.
2. Only a very small handful of respondents claimed to have seen the Princess of Wales, or knew others who had seen or met her. The following respondent (F46) records the impact of such an encounter: 'I was very fortunate to see her on two occasions. The one occasion I actually shook her hand and I shall always remember the excitement of it all and thinking I had shaken the hand of the future Queen!'
3. Episodes of *Casualty* are not infrequently rescheduled if story lines

are too similar to recent high-profile news stories of accidents or disasters.

4. Ang draws on the concept of 'structure of feeling' as devised by Raymond Williams (1977).

5. As will be seen in the next chapter, however, a quarter of all BFI respondents changed their opinions about Diana after she died.

3
The Grieving Masses?

As we saw in the last chapter, half of the BFI respondents claimed that the Princess of Wales's death had personally affected them in some way. As we also saw, the nature of this reaction was highly complex and it was hard to assess whether it constituted grief or a response to a disruption in normality. Nonetheless, the other half of the BFI sample was *not* personally affected by the princess's death. This is very significant because it runs counter to the media rhetoric at the time which had it that Britain was united in grief and counter to television and press images which depicted outpourings of this grief outside palaces in London. Yet when asked whether or not they had participated in the public mourning – by signing a condolence book or laying flowers, for example – the majority of respondents (70 per cent) denied that they had taken part in any way. This, too, seems to contradict the idea that Britain was effectively taking to the streets or participating in public mourning.

The aim of this chapter is to question the extent of 'public' mourning in the week following the princess's death and to explore the relationship between the television coverage and the active participation of members of the public in displays of grief. It will examine what respondents thought about the television coverage that week, whether or not they believed television influenced what they felt and the way they behaved, and what they thought of what they were witnessing. It will also examine the motivations and actions of those respondents who *did* participate, or who wanted to participate, and what this tells us about media involvement in constructing 'public' responses to crisis and the construction of 'public' events and rituals.

The Television Response: 1–5 September 1997

In the week between the accident and the funeral, the television schedules returned to a more normal and familiar pattern of output. With the exception of slightly extended news bulletins on BBC 1 on the Monday (1 September), including *Breakfast News*, most news broadcasts across the five terrestrial channels remained in their regular scheduled slots throughout the week. The few alterations to the schedules that week included a tribute programme on Monday evening on BBC 1 after the news, and the Queen's live address to the nation across all the terrestrial channels at 6 p.m. on the Friday before the funeral. Further tribute programmes were also shown on BBC 1 and ITV on that Friday night. The effect on the rest of the schedule was more subtle, as programmes were vetted to ensure that nothing was broadcast which might cause offence, a practice common after major disasters or highly publicised accidents. As a result, for example, an episode of the popular comedy *Only Fools and Horses* on the BBC was dropped because a character feigns a heart attack.[1] Television during the week did not return to the extensive 'marathonic' coverage that had characterised news output on the Sunday. Television was able to restore some degree of order and the disruption and distress was contained within the routine punctuation of news bulletins within the predictable and repetitive routines of the broadcast schedule.

Nonetheless, the death of the princess and its consequences continued to dominate the news output and became the focus of talk and magazine programmes such as *This Morning* (ITV) and a *Kilroy* special (BBC 1), as well as the breakfast-time programmes on BBC 1 and *GMTV*. There were several dominant strands in the television news coverage that week and, as with ordinary and routine news operations, these focused on conflict and the abnormal. The first revolved around the apparently unprecedented 'public' displays of grief, with cameras focused on the crowds of people flocking to London palaces and Harrods to lay flowers and leave messages, or queuing to sign condolence books. This will be discussed in subsequent sections of this chapter. The second major strand was the continued pursuit of the cause of the accident; news emerged on the Monday that the driver of the Mercedes Benz in which the princess had been killed was over the legal alcohol limit. This caused some ambiguity and took some of the sting out of accusations that had been levelled at the paparazzi and the tabloid press. This created, for the following respondent at least, some emotional turmoil.

My feelings kept swinging. I hated the paparazzi, then the driver, then not the driver. (F42)

This is consistent, to some degree, with Liebes's suggestion that the 'less possible it is to point to the actual villain, the less the chance of satisfactory resolution, and the more powerful the role of television in providing the framing' (1998, p. 74). Yet the role of the paparazzi in the accident was sustained with claims made that photographers had swarmed over the car after the accident, taking photographs and hampering the rescue operation. Seven photographers were charged with manslaughter.[2]

The third strand to the news narrative that week was the preparation for the funeral. Given Diana's ambiguous status, this was not technically to be a royal event, but, in the words of a 'Buckingham Palace' statement, 'a unique funeral for a unique person'. This created much speculation on a number of matters ranging from how the event should be staged to what route it should take, what songs would be sung to whom would be invited to attend the service at Westminster Abbey. News and discussion also focused on the institution of a one-minute silence, the closure of shops and businesses, and sporting cancellations as a mark of respect on the day of the funeral. There was much criticism at the beginning of the week, for example, of the Scottish Football Association (SFA), who had planned to hold a crucial World Cup qualifying match on the afternoon of the funeral. After mounting public and political pressure, the SFA was forced to back down and reschedule the fixture.

The final major strand to the news coverage was the growing criticism of the royal family. In the obituaries and biographies that appeared in the media following the princess's death, there was much emphasis on the unhappiness that had plagued her life; this inevitably referred to her conflict with the royal family. Yet the royal family not only looked bad for apparently giving her such a hard time, but also, by staying at Balmoral in Scotland for most of the week, they were deemed to be out of touch with public sentiment both emotionally and physically. This was exacerbated by the initial refusal to lower the Royal Standard to half-mast as a mark of respect for the princess.[3]

Responses to the Television Coverage of that Week

It is, of course, difficult to isolate responses to the television coverage from other media output that week. So intense was the interest in Diana that consumption of newspapers increased in the week following her death. *The Sun*, for example, 'reputedly' sold an extra million copies on the day following the accident, the *Daily Mail* an extra 700,000, and *The Guardian* saw sales rise by 20 per cent over the week. [4] Yet the vast majority of Tracking Study respondents claimed that television provided their main source of information.

Part of the reason for this is that Tracking Study viewers place more trust in television than in other media (Gauntlett and Hill, 1999). This led Gauntlett and Hill to suggest in the original study that 'there is something about watching TV news that people find more satisfying than other forms of news coverage' (1999, p. 53). As we saw in relation to the breaking news coverage of Diana's death, many respondents felt that television had truth claims above those of other forms of media. One viewer made this comparison for the week following the accident:

> *TV seemed to be more factual …. They didn't report the lies and rumours that came out that week, such as the surviving bodyguard losing his tongue and speculation like the* Daily Mail *did upon the Tuesday about Prince Charles's thoughts about the tragedy. How on earth do they know what he thinks!* (F26)

One possible explanation for the increased consumption of newspapers that week may have to do with the printed word as historical
evidence, compared to the transient and ephemeral nature of television broadcast output – as the following respondent perhaps
implies:

> *Even though I bought a newspaper everyday (as a keepsake, I suppose)*
> *I never really read them. So I got most of my information from*
> *television and radio. I think they were less intrusive than the press, but I*
> *felt I needed to know about everything.* (F32)

That television news provided most information that week should
come as no surprise, as this is consistent with various other studies
and previous news viewing practices recorded by Tracking Study
respondents. As previously referred to in Chapter 1, the Independent
Television Commission's report *Television: The Public's View* (1997)
stated that 94 per cent of those questioned used television generally
as a source of news compared to much lower proportions of 69 per
cent and 37 per cent for the press and radio, respectively. As Morrison (1992) also found in his study of the Gulf War, television was the
principal source of news, with 76 per cent of those surveyed saying
that television provided the 'best' coverage, compared to 10 per cent
saying radio and 7 per cent saying press. Furthermore, in the original
BFI study, Gauntlett and Hill found that respondents were, on the
whole, keen watchers of the television news, with 44 per cent, for
example, watching BBC television news more than twice a day. Thus,
if respondents regularly watch television news programmes, they are
likely to have had a high degree of exposure to the Diana coverage
in the week after the accident. Respondents were therefore well
qualified to cast their opinions and articulate their responses to the
television coverage that week.

As it turned out, there was a sharp rise in the number of respondents expressing increasing dissatisfaction with the television
coverage as the week progressed. By the end of that week, the number of respondents who were decidedly unhappy with the coverage

had almost doubled to around 40 per cent, while the numbers who had mixed feelings or who felt the coverage appropriate dropped to around 20 per cent and 40 per cent, respectively. This means that, one way or another, more than half of the BFI respondents were less than happy with the television coverage by the end of the week.

Significantly, these dissatisfied viewers do not necessarily correspond with the half of respondents who were *not* personally affected by the princess's death. On the one hand, there were some who were deeply upset by Diana's death, but were critical of aspects of the continuing television coverage; on the other, there were viewers less affected by events who expressed no complaint about the tone or level of coverage. For the most part, dissatisfied respondents were more likely to be critical of the way in which the Diana's death dominated the television news.

> *Diana's death upset me greatly. However, I became sick of the media coverage. It was much too much: every channel was the same except cable.* (F46)

> *... the entire broadcast media went into overkill on the story. The sensitivity shown when the news broke on Sunday was replaced by attempts to outdo each other and scoop a news item before a rival.* (M32)

In cases where Tracking Study viewers were regular news viewers, perhaps watching news bulletins more than once a day, it is conceivable that they reached saturation point quite quickly. At the same time, the death of Diana was highly symbolically and emotionally charged. As we saw in responses to the television coverage on the Sunday, many of those who were upset found the coverage too much to take in the end, craving some kind of relief by the end of the day. As the week wore on, the predominance of the event and its consequences in the news agenda may have emotionally exhausted some viewers even further. Yet, for those who had been unaffected by the princess's death, or who had been critical of the extensive coverage on the Sunday, it is likely that they would have become increasingly disinterested, bored or even frustrated by the continuing television news air time devoted to the event and its consequences.

> *If Sunday's coverage of the tragedy seemed excessive, it became increasingly unbearable in the six* [sic] *days up to the funeral on Saturday.* (M50)

In many cases, respondents simply wrote words or phrases such as 'excessive' or 'media overkill'. Criticism of apparent media 'overkill' is not an uncommon phenomenon and was recorded amongst audience responses to the Gulf War television coverage (Morrison, 1992). While the vast majority of Morrison's respondents were satisfied with the Gulf War coverage, dissatisfied viewers' biggest charge against television news was that it was repetitive and that too much air time was devoted to the war. This led Morrison to conclude: '

> Where it went wrong was 'over-selling' the war. Amongst those who registered dissatisfaction with how television covered the war, the general consensus would appear to be that it squeezed the story for everything that it was worth. (1992, p. 6)

Another criticism of the television coverage in the aftermath of the princess's death was that it was one-sided and, in the words of several respondents, made Diana out to be a 'saint'. On the Sunday of her death and in the week following, tribute programmes showed various film and video clips of the princess. These included clips of the princess enjoying a funfair ride with the princes, attending functions in stylish attire, walking through a minefield in Angola, touching an AIDS victim and sitting alone outside the Taj Mahal.

As Kitzinger has pointed out, many of the montages often used cinematic conventions such as soft focus, slow motion and music. These images 'carry a certain glamour, framing Diana in an angelic, "not of this world" light' (Kitzinger, 1998, p. 74). As one respondent noted:

I think TV very quickly conferred sainthood on Diana – even before
Elton John rewrote 'Candle in the Wind' it was being used as backing
music for a montage of images of her getting out of cars in slow motion
… (F27)

At the same time, this was complemented by tributes from the
great and the good who testified to Diana's sensitive and compassionate nature and spoke about her many charitable deeds. This
was further supported by tributes from members of the public who
had come into contact with the princess or had met her in the course
of her charity work. As the week progressed, there were many
reported instances of the princess having privately stayed in contact
with members of the public, of offering advice or consolation away
from the glare of publicity.

Such constructions are consistent with the Lawson's discussion of
'memorial broadcasting', which we discussed in Chapter 1. In the
conventions of everyday life, one should not 'speak ill of the dead'
and say only good things about the deceased. This convention was
something of which some Tracking Study respondents were aware
and to which they referred, perhaps implying media disingenuous-
ness and hypocrisy:

I had not appreciated the amount of work she had done and the effect
on so many. Most tributes boost the standing of the recently deceased
(even Jeffrey Bernard became the friend of many journalists who were
previously loathe to praise him).[5] *(M50)*

I've always felt pretty confused about her anyway – intrigued by my own
interest in her given that I disliked so much of what her fame stood for. I
hated the unabashed lauding of her – reminded me of the odd period
after Robert Maxwell died, when no one who had a bad word to say of
him could be found! (F47)

The following respondents have been quoted in full to provide a flavour of the complexity and vehemence of the criticism of the television tributes:

> *At first I thought I had misunderstood her and that there was a genuine side to her charity work and that she really did mind about unhappy people. Then, I thought, I am being 'conned' again. The interviews were presented as private little chats. But they were not one-to-one in private. The camera was there. Next, I wondered where those films came from. Were they originally shown as regional news items? The BBC were desperately trawling for any new, unfamiliar film of Diana – an understandable aim for a News Department. But these new 'films' all reinforced the saintly image of Diana. There was never any hint of another point of view, another interpretation of what she was doing. I came to the conclusion that the BBC was trying to please the public and feed them what they wanted – part of the Di-mania. I was left with the feeling that Diana was once again trying to manipulate me through television. I resented this as I resented the BBC editor's bias.* (F86)

> *I had a very low opinion of Diana as an individual, and as a public figure, but I did find myself beginning to wonder if I had been unjust in believing that the 'caring' was an act to seek attention … then I realised that I was being brainwashed, and remembered how much work for charity is done by other members of the Royal Family without ANY publicity seeking, and closed my ears.* (F71)

Nonetheless, not everyone was critical of this aspect of the television coverage. Many respondents felt that the biographies and tributes confirmed what they already knew, that she was a sensitive and compassionate person, deserving of the love and respect which people were now publicly demonstrating. Furthermore, just over a quarter of respondents, *mostly* women, actually claimed that watching the television news, tributes and biographies made them revise their opinion of the princess. This revision was predicated on prior prejudice against Diana because of reports they had seen or read about her in the past. As most people had never met her, their only knowledge of the princess would have been dependent on the media. Thus, irrespective of whether these people subscribed to tabloid or broadsheet news values, or exclusively television news, the chances are they would only have been exposed to the conflictual elements in Diana's life – the eating disorders, family strife, alleged affairs and 'kiss-and-tell-revelations' in the press and published biographies. As a result, some respondents were reminded of the unhappiness in the princess's life or were surprised to learn about her good work:

Before her death I really disliked Diana. I viewed her only as a clotheshorse, adulteress and drain on my money. This was despite the fact that I knew about her background and public duties. Because I watched so much TV I did change my opinion. I remembered that she had a very sad life and decided that through her charity work she did make a difference to many people. (F37)

I think I had more of an image of a jet-setter and of somebody who had lots of holidays and who argued with the Royal Family before the accident. The week's news coverage seemed to emphasise the excellent charity and campaigning work she did. I was also impressed by stories of how well she related to people 'on the edge' (e.g. homeless, aged, AIDS victims, refugees). So yes, the coverage emphasised that part of her life. It helped put it into focus and made me much more sympathetic to her. (M51)

While some respondents, mainly women again, also recognised that Diana was a complex and ambivalent person, the various narrative strands discussed in the previous chapter also ensured that the tribute programmes enhanced feelings of distress and guilt felt by other respondents. This is because the tributes and the biographies provided a melodramatic overview of her life which emphasised the tragedy of her death. Exacerbating feelings of guilt, the biographies highlighted the unhappy relationship between the princess and the media, thereby implicating the consumer with her death. At the same time, some respondents felt that they had not recognised Diana as a

good and compassionate person when she was alive, thereby deny-
ing her in life the love and respect she apparently deserved, as the
following suggest:

> *So, after her death, my eyes were opened to her goodness, and I cried*
> *tears inside for not seeing it when she was alive. It's a tragedy that she*
> *had to die for us to see that.* (F26)

> *The television coverage changed entirely my thoughts of Princess Diana.*
> *Prior to this, I had no opinion of her, neither good nor bad. But when*
> *we were shown all the good things she did for people who needed help –*
> *some of the outcasts of society – I admired her and felt ashamed of*
> *myself.* (F75)

The other aspect of the television coverage which respondents were
critical of that week were the scenes of people laying flowers, leaving messages and queuing to sign condolence books. This is because
people found the public scenes of grieving distasteful, or were hor-
rified by the apparent 'mass hysteria' sweeping the streets of
London. In the following sections, we will look at whether or not
Tracking Study respondents participated in these events and the significance of the media depictions of 'public' mourning. As will be
seen, the relationship between television and the public outpourings
is a highly complex one.

Non-participation
The majority of Tracking Study respondents (70 per cent) did not
participate in any public or private displays of grief for the Princess
of Wales. While this might yield no initial surprise, remembering that
half of the sample was not profoundly affected, this situation is again
a complex one where unaffected respondents did participate while
deeply distressed ones did not.

While respondents were not asked why they did *not* participate,
several reasons were offered. First, there were those respondents
who were not affected by the princess's death and who were simply

not moved to participate in any way. Secondly, there were those who would like to have participated, but due to infirmity, age or lack of time, were unable to do so. There were also some cases where respondents felt that they would have liked to participate, but simply never summoned up the energy, as the following two respondents suggest:

> *I didn't sign a book of condolence because the queues put me off. If my computer hadn't been packed in a box I would have visited the website.* (M25)

> *We intended to go and sign a book of condolence at Guildford Cathedral but never got there. I'm sure my excuse was suitably poor.* (F18)

There were a number of respondents who were surprised, baffled or outraged by the apparent scenes of 'public' mourning. Again, this is perhaps not surprising considering that half of all the BFI's respondents were not personally affected by the princess's death. For one respondent, for example, the public response seemed to imply a lack of priorities on the part of the mourners:

> *It's a pity that there is not such a public showing of grief for all those servicemen who died in two world wars and subsequent engagements. After all they were victims of circumstances over which they had no control.* (M46)

Those baffled or surprised by the apparent displays of grief also include people who had been upset by the princess's death. This is perhaps because some found the scenes in some way distasteful – not the proper way to behave when someone dies (Walter, 1999b). For many people, death and grief are taboo subjects. Charting the changes in attitudes towards death in western society since the Middle Ages, Phillippe Ariès has suggested that, in modern times, death has become sequestrated from everyday life. Whereas, once, people died at home in the bosom of their family, death now occurs in distinct and separate institutions away from public life, such as hospitals and residential centres for the elderly (Ariès, 1976). Indeed, these institutions are a constituent feature of modernity because they try to extend life and keep death at bay (Bauman, 1992); death is itself a challenge to modernity (Mellor, 1993). This is why Doane argues that catastrophe is an important aspect of television news because it strikes right at the heart of societies underpinned by technology (1990).

As we saw in the last chapter, Diana's death in a senseless car accident exactly undermines that sense of security which modern technology provides. No one is safe, even an important person like the Princess of Wales can be killed prematurely. People are uncomfortably reminded of their own mortality. As a result, death has become a taboo subject in modern society, described by Baudrillard as 'incurable deviance' (cited from Gane, 1991), the ultimate faux pas. Grief is an embarrassment and '[s]orrow does not inspire pity but repugnance.' (Ariès, 1976, p. 90).

It has been suggested, however, that the advent of AIDS in the 1980s has given death a higher profile in the media than at any other peace-time period in the twentieth century (Davies, 1996). Nonetheless, Hockey has argued that it is still not socially acceptable to grieve in public in the United Kingdom (1997), although this may be giving way to social change and an emerging clash between those with stiff-upper-lip attitudes and those who want to talk about bereavement (Walter, 1999b). Older respondents in the BFI Tracking Study, especially perhaps the males, might well fall into the 'stiff-upper-lip' camp. As Walter has noted, the elderly tend to be more stoical (1999b), as demonstrated by the respondent (M74) who stated that: 'Mourning is a private thing.'

Participation and Precedent

Thirty per cent of respondents participated in the 'public' mourning. Participation can take many forms; the types recorded by these respondents were the laying of flowers, either in London or an appropriate local site; visiting London palaces; signing books of condolence; sending a letter or message to a newspaper; specially attending church; or sending an e-mail and visiting the royal website. It is significant, however, that most of these respondents responded locally or in a place, time and manner of convenience. It was only those who lived near London who actually visited the palaces where the public mourning was depicted. Participation locally can be simply accounted for by the geographical spread of respondents around the country, but this does have further implications which we will return to later.

When asked whether the television coverage had influenced the desire of these respondents to participate, the vast majority simply said 'no'. In some cases, this was emphasised by large letters or exclamation marks, or accompanied by qualifying comments stating that they had wanted to participate in any case. Yet this picture is also complex and contradictory. As stated in the last section, there were many who were profoundly affected by the princess's death who did not participate. Curiously, there were conversely those who *did* participate in the public displays of grief, but who were not themselves that deeply upset about the princess's death. This is something to which we will also return.

From early on the Sunday morning that the princess died, people started to lay flowers or leave messages outside Buckingham Palace, Kensington Palace and even Harrods in London. These people were not responding to media images. In asking 'Who placed the first flower?' (1998, p. 83), Silverstone argues that media critics and scholars forget the importance of personal experience, and that real people wanted to commemorate the Princess of Wales. The identifications and connections that people made with the princess 'were acted upon. They were performed. The ritual was being invented in real time. And public space was being occupied. You could smell the lilies' (ibid., p. 84).

Such reactions were not unprecedented, but echoed responses to other tragic events, either public or private. Indeed, it is customary for people to lay flowers or messages at the scene or site of someone's death, such as at the site of road accidents, and flowers are often displayed outside houses in working-class areas on the day of a funeral (Richardson, 1999). Furthermore, people are increasingly taking matters into their own hands to create their own rituals of mourning or participating in informal or idiosyncratic funerary services (Richardson, 1999; Francis et al., 1999). As a result, this has extended to major accidents and disasters. Flowers were seen near the site, for example, of the Kings Cross underground fire, laid on the sea by the bereaved following the Zeebrugge ferry disaster, and on the bank of the River Thames following the *Marchioness* river boat accident (Richardson, 1999). On the Sunday morning following the Hillsborough football stadium disaster, members of the public were already waiting outside Hillsborough and Anfield football grounds to leave flowers and scarves. In the week following the Hillsborough disaster, it is estimated that one million people, more than the entire population of Liverpool, filed through the gates at Anfield to pay their respects. Many of these had to queue for as long as six hours to gain entry to the stadium (Walter, 1991).

Walter suggests that the public response to the Hillsborough football stadium disaster arose out of a unique combination of factors. The disaster involved young people, which heightened the sense of tragedy. It involved football, which has almost religious connotations for many people. It involved fans of the Liverpool team – and Liverpool is a city where there is a particularly strong connection with football. It was also significant that Liverpool has a large working-class and Roman Catholic population, and this meant that many of the informal and public responses were devised from Irish death rituals (Walter, 1991). Such informal and working-class rituals as those seen at Anfield may have been perceived as 'abnormal' or unusual by a middle-class media. Nonetheless, this behaviour may have provided an aspirational model for middle-class people around the country who wanted to move away from stoical and solitary responses to bereavement, but who lacked the same sense of community to do so (Walter, 1991).

The media depiction of mourning following major disasters may therefore be part of a longer term shift in cultural and social values and behaviours – a shift from the stiff upper lip to a more emotional and communal response – although the actual pace of change may still be slow. In many circles, it is still unacceptable for people to grieve in public, even at funerals (Hockey, 1997). As a result, for some sections of society where grieving is experienced in private, behind closed doors, media representations of bereavement can carry significant force because people do not know how or when to conduct that grieving (Walter, Littlewood, and Pickering, 1995).

Drawing on this work, Hockey suggests that such images of bereavement mark out 'extraordinary' events such as child murders or disasters as occasions when it is acceptable to grieve in public, and that such images often focus on crying women (1997). Indeed, members of the public, as media consumers, may have recognised that the Princess of Wales's death was one of those occasions. As Ghosh has observed:

> ... anyone who had watched the coverage of the death of the murdered
> black teenager Stephen Lawrence, or the Liverpool toddler Jamie
> Bulger, or of the Scottish schoolchildren massacred in Dunblane, knew
> exactly what the conventions were regarding cellophane and messages ...
> (1998, p. 43)

As a result, any cultural and social changes in mourning practice may be the result of cumulative practical experiences and media discourses. In some instances, this slow change *may* have been accelerated in the week that the Princess of Wales died, and this is something we will return to later.

While wanting to mourn in some way or commemorate the princess, the lack of experience of bereavement may have left many unsure as to what to do. At the same time, this uncertainty may have been increased by the princess's ambiguous status and because the accident took place abroad, which might have meant that people were unsure about where flowers should be sent or left (Richardson, 1999). As Walter notes, at times of stress or uncertainty, people take their cues from others around them (1999a). As a result, the positive media images of flowers outside the palaces probably did exert an influence. As will be seen, however, the depiction of crowds at particular sites may have exemplified an aspirational social experience, exaggerated the extent of the public reaction and normalised the mourning responses.

Communitas and Pilgrimage

As suggested, there were those who participated in the public out-pourings, but who did not claim to be personally affected by the princess's death. This is also complicated by the fact that one in ten of all respondents said that the television coverage *did* make them *want* to take part in the public response, although not all of these actually did. It is therefore important here to make a clear separation between the emotional responses to the princess's death and the actual participation in the public displays. Respondents themselves did not necessarily make this separation and it is inevitable that the relationship between the two is complex. By separating the two here, however, it becomes possible to better understand the apparent public response and the media relationship to it.

For those who wanted to participate, but were not actually profoundly affected by Diana's death, it is possible that they may have wanted to be part of, or were drawn to be part of, a wider collective experience. What supports this possibility is that many said it was the images of the crowds in London that motivated or attracted involvement. This is suggested by the following two respondents, who live in London:

> *I did get a strong urge to go down to the Palace to feel the mood after seeing the images on TV and I did more than once.* (M25)

> *I went to St James's Palace to look. This was based on the television coverage of the flower laying. I found it very difficult and unexpectedly moving. I would have gone to Kensington Palace, but it was too difficult for me to find the time to go to both. I did feel a strong pressure to conform to the public mood mostly initiated by the media coverage and the feeling that this was a one-off phenomenon.* (F31)

Yet those who said they wanted to join the crowds or visit London included people who did not, in the end, manage to attend or participate.

> *I wanted to go to London to be one of the many. I wanted to make my statement too, and when I saw how many people felt the same there was a sort of compulsion – even a sense of guilt at not just getting up and going, but of thinking of reasons why it perhaps wasn't practical.* (F48)

What these respondents are referring to here is not grief or mourning, but a compulsion to attend, to 'feel the mood', to see for themselves. This 'mood' is particularly significant because in the wake of the princess's death there was widespread media rhetoric about the apparent public response, with phrases and concepts such as 'unity in grief', 'the people', 'the People's Princess' and the 'nation mourns' being widely thrown around. At the same time, as we will discuss in the following sections, television images framed the public response in such a way as to support, or complement, this rhetoric; this reaffirmed or reified notions of the social, the collective, the community and the nation state. In the week Diana died, this rhetoric and these images had a particular potency and resonance.

The death of Diana was symbolically very disruptive. As we discussed in the previous chapter, the death of someone close (or who is perceived to be close) can lead to existential crisis and a loss of confidence in the beliefs, practices and patterns of everyday life (Mellor, 1993). Davies (1999) and Couldry (1999) have both argued that the disruption caused by the princess's death led to a period of what the anthropologist Victor Turner would describe as *liminality*.

Originating from the Latin word *limen* meaning 'threshold', liminal states are marginal and transitory, they are 'neither here nor there; they are betwixt and between the positions assigned and arrayed by law, custom, convention, and ceremonial' (Turner, 1969, p. 95). The characteristics of liminality, for Turner, are 'necessarily ambiguous', and in the suspension and confusion of everyday social structures and hierarchies they can allow for a wide variety of practical and symbolic responses. Such responses include the transgression of rules, laws and conventions, and, as a result, they constitute a threat to the social and moral order. They are dangerous and disturbing.

Liminal situations arise in circumstances which include 'rites of passage', when an individual or group undergoes a transformation in their social status (Turner, 1969), such as initiation into a social group, marriage and, significantly here, death. Liminal situations also arise in what Turner describes as social dramas (1982). In what again highlights the complex interrelationship between lived experience, life narrative and media narrative, Turner argues that social dramas are characterised by disruption to the normal social fabric, followed by a period of crisis, then a ceremonial or administrative redress that either resolves conflict or recognises schism. Echoing Geraghty's description of the classic narrative, equally characterised by disruption, crisis and resolution (1998), the period of crisis constitutes that period of liminality when things are in a state of change or flux.

It should be evident here that the period of liminality which followed in the wake of Diana's death is consistent both with the change of social status which individuals undergo in 'rites of passage' and the wider crisis reported in the media. What differentiates liminality in the rites of passage from the liminality in the social drama is that, in the first, it can be characterised by an extraordinary *bonding* within the community, while, in the second, it is marked by *conflict* within the community. Both elements of bonding and conflict were visible in the wake of Diana's death and this contributed to the highly charged atmosphere.

It is, perhaps, this bonding experience to which BFI respondents aspired when they wanted to join the scenes and crowds depicted on television. Described by Turner as *communitas*, this bonding is a particular kind of social relationship distinct from everyday, mundane experiences of community (1969). This relationship is characterised by equality because the breakdown of ordinary social codes, classifications and practices inherent in liminal phenomena offers the possibility of 'homogeneity and comradeship' (Turner, 1969, p. 96).

'It is rather a matter of giving recognition to an essential and generic human bond, without which there would be no society' (ibid., p. 97). The concept of *communitas* is particularly compelling when considering public responses to the death of Diana because mortality touches everyone and bereavement is no respecter of class or status. Death, in popular parlance, is 'the great leveller'. As a result, people who were profoundly affected in the wake of the princess's death had a common bond, irrespective of their social standing. Just as the recognition of emotional realism implicit in *Dallas*, discussed in the last chapter, cut through class and cultural boundaries, so did the emotional experience of the death of Diana.

This is particularly significant as emotional experience is a key constituent in the emergence of *communitas* because it is free of structural ties which, Turner asserts, are essentially cognitive and grounded in classification and hierarchy (1969). Yet this recourse to emotion is perhaps also closely related to Ang's conceptualisation of the melodramatic imagination. Implicit in the humbling and emotional comradeship of *communitas* is the recognition of powerlessness, weakness and inferiority in the face of the cognitive and coercive powers of social structure. Thus, responding publicly to the death of Diana, participants are perhaps explicitly recognising that shared powerlessness.

This recognition was further emphasised in the wake of Diana's death by those who felt marginalised (such as women, gays or members of ethnic minorities) and who identified with the princess's own marginality and ambiguous status outside the royal family – 'someone who is like us but not like us'. This had even further resonance when public and media tributes lauded the princess's stand on behalf of the weak, infirm and dispossessed. Such processes of *communitas* evoke, especially from the position of weakness and marginality, a subjunctive mode of culture (Turner, 1977), thoughts of what a better world might look like, as the following respondents suggest:

> ... *it was all very strange. There was a sense of love, solemnity, goodness and change all in the air at once.* (F26)

It was as if a safety valve had been suddenly and unexpectedly released and we were allowed to let off steam and emotion – for a brief moment, it was OK to feel in a society which is noted for its allegiance to the 'stiff upper lip'. Fragility and female values led the mood of the nation for a time. (F36)

Why did these respondents necessarily want to join the crowds in person? The media, especially television, has the power to connect disparate people, events and places. Many of the same Tracking Study respondents had previously discussed this important aspect of television, with many describing it as 'a window on the world' (Gauntlett and Hill, 1999). This is what has been described by Harvey as *time–space* compression where telecommunications can shrink the world to a 'global village' by linking different places and time zones (1989). It is because of such processes that Dayan and Katz (1992), drawing on the work of Shils and Young (1953), suggest that media events such as the Princess of Wales's funeral can connect the centre of society to its periphery. People watching from the privacy of their own homes can be connected to a wider public domain and people from the furthest reaches of the nation can be equally connected. This is achieved, they argue, 'not only through the experience of *communitas*, but through direct communion with central symbols and values ...' and as a result 'the mass audiences of television events partially overcome their dispersion and atomization' (1992, p. 196).

There is a problem here. This is not least because the television pictures of the crowds in London, in news reports and live links, did *not* constitute a media event according to Dayan and Katz's definition.[6] Where analyses such as Harvey's and Dayan and Katz's appear to go wrong is in forgetting or obscuring the very *mediated* quality of the media. In what Thompson calls *space–time distanciation*, symbolic forms are detached from the context of their production and transmitted into different contexts in a one-way process. As a result:

... mass communication institutes a fundamental break between the producer and the receiver, *in such a way that recipients have relatively little capacity to intervene in the communicative process and contribute to its course and content.* (Thompson, 1990, p. 15; Thompson's emphasis)

Furthermore, as Ellis (1982) has argued, television involves the delegation of 'the look' to a participant (the one who holds the camera) at the scene of the event. This means that:

[t]he process of the delegation of the look leaves the TV viewer in a position of isolation rather than separation from the events shown. The sense of complicity with the audience presented by broadcast TV tends to intensify this isolation. The viewer is at home; TV presents things that come from outside the home. (Ellis, 1982, p. 165)

Thus it should be argued that, although television involves symbolic content, it is itself an institutional and structural barrier which separates actors from that fundamental experience of *communitas*. Actual participation in that *communitas* would have to involve physical proximity to other people in liminal spaces.

Yet where were people going to find this unmediated experience of *communitas*? As previously suggested, most of the BFI respondents who did participate did so locally. This is consistent with Marion Bowman's account of what happened in Bath where 'some of the activity was similar to, if on a smaller scale than, London' (1999, pp. 215–16). People attended a memorial service, for example, and left flowers outside Bath Abbey. In particular, Bowman noted a phenomenon which she describes as 'shop window shrines' where proprietors of cafés and shops had installed a picture, flowers or candles in memory of the princess. Shops and cafés (whether they be newsagents or supermarkets, down-market eateries or swanky brasseries), libraries and town halls represent the mundane, ordinary and everyday spaces of the high street. In effect what Durkheim would describe as a profane world (1915). Thus these sites of individual mourning may be devoid of the liminality and thus the intense experience of social bonding which *communitas* offers. As Marc Augé has argued, in a world in which people are increasingly spending their time in or in transit through 'non-places', such as motorways, supermarkets, car parks and cash dispensers, there is perhaps little scope for any kind of sociality (1995).

For those BFI respondents who claimed that the television coverage made them feel that they wanted to participate, it was in London that they wanted to join the crowds. It was there that the television images were depicting an intense social experience. This should come as no surprise, as London is the principal site of royalty in the United Kingdom. Yet this may also have helped add a liminal dimension to the mourning because Diana was no longer, technically, a member of the royal family. It was this ambiguity, and the fact that she died outside the country, that led initial mourners to centre on empty buildings in London (Davies, 1999). Nonetheless, the intimation of royalty is also crucial to understanding how London is central to the social experience in the wake of the princess's death.

Drawing on Emile Durkheim's seminal work, *The Elementary Forms of the Religious Life* (1915), Harris argues that the monarchy is set apart and sacred, and therefore represents the social totality:

> A central argument in the Elementary Forms is that the superposited, intrinsic quality of sacredness is the result of the fact that sacred things symbolize a totality whose reality transcends that of the individuals which compose it. Sacred signifiers are sacred because the sacred is just such a reality, namely 'Society'. (Harris, 1999, p. 102)

This means that the London palaces themselves became highly charged symbolic and sacred sites, and, in the aftermath of the princess's death, the centres of pilgrimage. The streets around the London palaces were, in effect, sacred places where intense social bonding could be seen to be both experienced and symbolically celebrated.

Yet the media framing of London sites as sacred places simultaneously undermined the possibility of direct experience because it

emphasised the provincial exclusion (Harris, 1999) and the isolation
of the viewer (Ellis, 1982). This is because people are usually not conscious of the spatial separation identified by Thompson (1990)
between media production and reception (Couldry, 1999). As a
result, meeting a celebrity or attending a place of media production
has special value. This has led Couldry to suggest that Diana's death
'intensified the inherent asymmetry in the celebrity situation' (1999,
p. 81). People became conscious of the 'fundamental break' between
production and reception. On one hand, most people had never met
Diana and now they never would; on the other hand, they were now
doubly aware that they could never even have hoped to meet her, to
occupy the same space that she did or to join the crowds. The following respondent poignantly demonstrated this exclusion from the
centre of royal and celebrity space:

> *As soon as I saw people making their pilgrimages to St James,*
> *Buckingham and Kensington palaces upon the Monday and Tuesday*
> *after Princess Diana's death, I wanted to do that but couldn't because I*
> *didn't have the money to do so. But if I did, I would have went down*
> *there even though I'd never visited the capital in my life.* (F26)

As television provided a glimpse of intense social activity, *communitas* in a sacred place, it ultimately taunted this respondent because
she is economically and geographically excluded from participation
in the 'public' mourning spaces. Nonetheless, the desire to participate
in an unmediated experience of *communitas* and to visit a site of
sacred and special value remained.

By responding to these television images in this way, respondents
may have been expressing a desire to cross that boundary between
media production and reception. As Couldry has suggested, people
signing condolence books and laying flowers with messages for other
members of the public to read were effectively taking centre stage.
'Non-media people' were allowed to become actors in 'what is purely
a "symbolic reversal" of the media's power' (Couldry, 1999, p. 80).
This was a desire to go beyond Baudrillardian simulation and the

emptiness of spectacle to experience something real. In Silverstone's terms, this was an example of real people in the real world wanting to occupy public space and 'smell the flowers' (1998). Like MacCannell's 'tourist', they wanted to find authenticity and commune with a wider social totality (1989). It is thus significant that they wanted to join with other people in explicitly socialised space. As a consequence, the motivation to visit London may not so much have been a matter of media effects, but of media *inadequacy*, the inability of the media to overcome time and space to provide physical proximity to a first-order social or sacred experience.

Reality Effects and the Frame of Disaster

What clearly emerges from BFI respondents, however, is the dissonance between television depictions of public grief and actual emotions and behaviour. As we have seen, half of the BFI respondents were not personally affected by the princess's death. Of those who were affected, it is difficult to assess the extent to which people actually felt 'grief' or whether their emotional reactions constituted a response to the disruption of normality and vulnerability in the face of mortality. Furthermore, the majority of respondents did not participate in any of the 'public' outpourings of 'grief'. When they did participate, it was usually somewhere local, at a place of convenience or in an otherwise untelegenic manner, such as writing messages to newspapers or sending an e-mail. Yet all this seems to stand in stark contrast to the media rhetoric of 'unity in grief' and to the images on television, and in the press, of people crying, of crowds adding to the mountains of flowers and queuing for hours to sign condolence books, particularly in London. This raises some fundamental questions. How did television images depict or construct such notions of public grief and how was this conveyed as a unified response? As well as depicting a sense of *communitas*, what other consequences did this have?

A template for 'grief' was perhaps constructed in the televisual frame of disaster which followed in the immediate aftermath of the princess's death. Focusing on crisis and conflict, the frame of disaster calls for 'people who scream the most' (Liebes, 1998, p. 80). On that Sunday, television news brought pictures of people starting to congregate around London palaces, some in tears and some caught on camera angry at the press. Yet, as suggested previously, the initial focus on members of the public laying flowers and leaving messages on the day of the accident conformed to generic conventions of paying tribute to a deceased person. It also substituted for the lack of a visual centre to the story and provided a much-needed filler of air time as television news went to 'marathonic' coverage.

As the week progressed, however, the public response became a major news story in its own right. In just the same way that the response in Liverpool to the Hillsborough stadium disaster was considered unusual by middle-class journalists (Walter, 1991), and thus newsworthy, so, too, was the apparently 'unprecedented' displays of public mourning for Diana. The 'people' also became major actors in the social drama because the apparent public emotion offered an alternative position to the stiff-upper-lip royals who had been, according to the tributes, complicit in Diana's misery. This apparent disjunction between 'the people' and the royal family was emphasised in the media and the public response was read as a direct challenge to the authority of monarchy.

Such promotion of antagonism is a common feature of day-to-day news reporting because journalists 'are afraid to be boring, they opt for confrontations over debates, prefer polemics over rigorous argument, and in general do whatever they can to promote conflict' (Bourdieu, 1998, pp. 3–4). This does not mean that journalists are not working in good faith, or that they are consciously elaborating fictions, but that, as Bourdieu argues, they are working within a set of pre-existing conventions and practices. In any news situation, the journalist is under pressure – he or she has to think fast. The way to work quickly is to think in clichés, or Flaubert's 'received ideas' (Bourdieu, 1998). As a result, journalists are working with 'predigested' thoughts, things which make sense, are self-evident or obvious. In times of disaster or trauma, these practices are particularly effective because journalists are under even greater pressure than usual to come up with the goods. During news situations, whether they be a strike, a riot or, in this instance, mourners in the Mall, television and press journalists focus on those who are the most photogenic, the most verbally or visually articulate, to convey the main essence of the news story. So, even in the liminal period following Diana's death, television news conventions still sought out 'people who scream the most'. In other words, they focused on heartfelt messages attached to flowers and people who were visibly emotionally affected. Indeed, this is exactly what one respondent (M49) noted: 'I felt the TV focused on more extrovert displays of grief.'

At the same time, interviews with members of the public who had travelled to London from different parts of the country and the more telegenic aspects of the apparent grief were presented as signifying a wider response. At a rhetorical level, this was constituted in the news by phrases and concepts such as 'the people', 'the people's princess' and 'public mourning', and was complexly interwoven with discourses of public celebrity, royalty and nationhood. It was also read as an important national event because it was broadcast on national television. Yet television's ability to construct a unified public response is usefully and succinctly described by Jenny Kitzinger (1998, p. 77):

> While the 'nation in mourning' was represented in all the media coverage, it was television images which most insistently presented a 'seamless unity in grief'. Self-consciously employing the double meaning of contemplation and imagery, BBC news bulletins used a compilation tape called 'Diana reflections'. The tape showed familiar scenes from her life, intercut with a singing choirboy, and soundbites from representatives of different charities. It concluded by cutting between the different interviewees as each spoke, as if with one voice, a consecutive line from a prayer (BBC, 'Diana reflections', 5 September 1997). Elsewhere the cameras displayed the close-up shots of weeping faces, often then pulling back to show a massive crowd. The impression was that everyone was in grief, that everyone was in tears.

Thus the media was able to create what Bourdieu, following French literary critics, describes as a *reality effect* (1998). Television gave the impression, as Kitzinger describes, that *everyone* was mourning, that everyone was crying. As a result, this led Walter to suggest, 'Viewers at home could be forgiven for believing that everyone out there was crying and hugging – except perhaps themselves, which may be how so many were made to feel so odd.' (1999b, p. 25)

Indeed, given that so many of the BFI's respondents were not affected by the princess's death and that so many did not participate, it should come as no surprise that some respondents felt excluded or marginalised by what they saw on television. At the same time, people *were* personally affected by the princess's death, so the responses of people around some of the respondents who felt marginalised appeared to confirm the rhetoric of grief. In some instances, respondents recorded disagreements with friends, colleagues, family or other household members in the aftermath of the princess's death. This left some feeling beleaguered and even guilty:

> *I have been made to feel guilty for expressing my feelings and for not signing a book of condolence, by people who had never met the princess. I dread to think how these people cope with the death of someone close to them.* (F27)

> *My wife Sally's response was quite surprising, she was truly upset, watching everything on television, reading voraciously, at times accusing me of being deliberately distant about the events, just to be 'different'. I found and still do find it hard to explain my less than emotional response to the event.* (M49)

Yet a significant proportion of respondents (around 15 per cent), predominantly ones who had not been affected by the princess's death, suggested that media images had another negative consequence. Combined with the tribute programmes on television (which, as we saw, influenced the opinions of a quarter of Tracking Study respondents), images of public participation in the media were blamed by these respondents for whipping up 'mass hysteria' or 'Diana-mania'.

> *I think it was partly wound up by the media telling them how they should be affected. Showing people weeping at the scene of laying flowers, appealing to mass hysteria. It was an opportunity to participate in national breast-beating – not all those people can possibly have had a personal experience of Diana.* (F41)

In a handful of cases, respondents saw more alarming parallels:

> *It is a little frightening when I think of seeing the pictures of Stalin's death. The whole of Red Square packed with weeping crowds. Or the masses that applauded Hitler … That's where TV is dangerous if it overdoes its coverage.* (F72)

> *It depresses me that so many people can be manipulated, and that the media can compel so much conformity by reiterating only one viewpoint (nation united in grief, the most wonderful woman who ever lived, a great loss to the whole world). You can see how easily it was worked under Stalin and Hitler: anybody who doesn't agree had best keep quiet.* (M63)

By concentrating on what was unusual and abnormal, therefore, journalistic conventions constructed public unity in grief. This made some people, both mourners and sceptics alike, think that everyone else was out there. It gave the impression that most of the British public was grief-stricken, even though this may not have been the case.

The Frame of Ritual and Normative *Communitas*

The question that therefore arises here is whether or not the mourning and *communitas* depicted on television was illusory. This question becomes even more significant when accounts by writers and academics warn us not to take the depictions of public mourning around London at face value.

In the first instance, numerous commentators, including Walter (1999b) and O'Hear (1998), reported that people were not hysterical or wailing. People at the London sites tended to be quiet and subdued. Presumably, therefore, not everyone was tearful. Secondly, there is some question as to the actual composition of these crowds and whether or not they reflected all elements of a wider society in grief. Part of the problem here is the contradictory nature of some of these accounts. According to McKibbon, for example, 'the population as a whole seemed fairly well represented', although the queues were 'understandably biased towards the hale and hearty' (1998, p. 18). On the other hand, Merck (summarising various reports and commentators) referred to the 'rich vein of Tory tabloid readers' and to the metropolitan character of the crowds, namely Londoners (1998). This is similarly echoed by Walter, who suggests that the people around the palaces tended to be youngish female adults, *Daily Mail* readers, women with children and a disproportionate amount of gays and blacks. As a result, '"the people", Diana's people, were not synonymous with the British people' (Walterb, 1999, p. 30). Nonetheless, he adds that, because the groups attending the sites around London were 'sufficiently diverse', they became confused with the British people. At the same time, as Merck and McKibbon stated, there were also a lot of foreign tourists:

> There seemed to be a considerable number of tourists both in the queue, Americans particularly, and in the crowd, where a great many Italians and Spaniards were taking photographs … The number of photo-seekers around Buckingham Palace was so large that the police had created photography only queues. (McKibbon, 1998, pp. 18–19)

The time of year, and place, may also have had an impact on who attended these sites. This is because, as Ghosh suggests, 'Diana's death occurred at the end of the school and summer holidays – a time when "real" news stories are at a discount, and one of the latest periods in the year when an open-air carnival in London is still feasible' (1998, p. 43). As a result, Ghosh goes on to add that 'it would have been extraordinary if it had *not* happened' (Ghosh's emphasis). Given the metropolitan and tourist bias, and given that, as we have seen, people wanted to have a look, 'feel the mood' and participate in a wider social experience, the important point here is simply that not everyone attending these sites was necessarily grief-stricken by the princess's death. Different people may have been there for different reasons.

Yet the depiction of *communitas* and public mourning in the streets of London by television and other media was not necessarily chimeric or illusory. There are several complexly interwoven reasons for this. Walter suggests, for example, that different visitors to the London sites assumed different roles at different times. Noting that some people were probably in London as tourists and attended what was to become a tourist attraction, while others went to participate in a historic event, Walter (1999b, p. 35) asserts:

> Crucially, many individuals played more than one of these roles. The tourist became strangely moved and became a mourner. The mourner wanted to be part of a historical event and brought her camera along.

Just as tourists are moved at memorial sites, but found laughing in the bar afterwards, Walter argues, the people around the streets of London behaved as they normally would at 'emotionally charged sites to do with the death of heroes' (ibid.). Such a response is perhaps evidence of the transformative dimension of liminality, where roles are inverted or changed. At the same time, similarly diverse phenomena have been noted at other sacred centres, sites of pilgrimage and places of special value.

As previously suggested, liminal spaces allow for a variety of symbolic and practical responses. Eade and Sallnow argue, for example, that attendance at sacred shrines is characterised by competing values and discourses. As such, pilgrimage sites provide 'a ritual space for the expression of a diversity of perceptions and meanings which the pilgrims themselves bring to the shrine and impose on it' (1991, p. 10). As a result, there is often mutual misunderstanding amongst the visitors and participants at these places. In just the same way, Diana in life had meant different things to different people at different times. In death, she equally became a 'contested sphere' in which different agencies and individuals negotiated claims and counter-claims as to who she was and what she represented (Hughes-Freeland and Crain, 1998). This does not mean, however, that the sacred qualities and social inclusivity of such sites of contestation are in any way diminished.

What makes these places sacred is the way in which they are sep-arated from the mundane, everyday profane world. As we saw above, it was the media framing of London sites that marked them out as liminal and sacred. Yet it was not just the depiction on screen that marked them out as liminal, but also the actual presence of television cameras which demarcated physical spaces for those in attendance. According to Becker, the media marks out public events, such as the personalised rites performed by individuals around London palaces, by distinguishing them from ordinary, day-to-day events. The media also contributes to the 'internal structure' of such rituals by selecting and recording specific aspects of them and separating them from their surroundings (1995, 1998). It selects 'peak moments' which con-dense the whole meaning of the event (Becker, 1995). Such moments in the wake of Diana's death, for example, could include the actual moment of individual flower laying. At the same time, the media at such events record the 'general atmosphere', the 'various activities that constitute the event and its boundaries' (ibid., p. 639), and the range of people there, with particular emphasis on 'star performers'. In short, media presence at public events or rituals temporally and spatially frames and legitimates the experience for those in atten-dance. Following the death of Diana, the media frame transformed certain 'public spaces into arenas for performance, and authenticated the significance of specific acts within those spaces' (Becker, 1998, p. 91). As a result, those standing (in the spaces) in front of the cam-eras, irrespective of who they were or their motivations to attend, were effectively transformed by the media frame into mourners. Not only was the visitor transformed for the spectator watching at home, but for him or herself. The act of attendance itself became an act of (correct) performance with both other participants and the media bearing witness.

There is also a temporal dimension to the way these events were framed which needs to be touched upon here. Becker argues that the media framing of ritual is a reflexive process and this has consequences for how people behave at such events. Constituting a historical record of a given event, both institutionally and in personal memory, '[I]ndividuals refer to these records when they consider and plan their participation in a later cultural performance' (Becker, 1995, p. 642). Indeed, responses to previous public and personal tragedies may have provided an automatic model for spontaneous participation in demonstrations of grief in the immediate hours following the princess's death. The television coverage of public participation spanned the period of a week, however, and some felt a desire to join these scenes after witnessing them on television. What we have suggested here is that these respondents may have been motivated to participate in the intense social experience of *communitas*. Such *communitas* emerges in liminal spaces where rules, structures and hierarchies have been suspended or thrown into confusion following traumatic occurrences such as death.

Yet Turner differentiates between two types of *communitas* (1978). The first, 'spontaneous *communitas*', is what we have previously described. It is direct and immediate, and there is something special and 'magical' about it. It is a profound form of social interaction. It is perhaps this type of *communitas* to which some aspired in the liminal period following the princess's death. The second type of *communitas* Turner refers to as 'normative'. This is where a subculture or group tries to sustain the conditions of spontaneous *communitas*. This is, as Turner asserts, to 'denature itself' because *communitas* cannot be legislated or normalised. Organised or prescribed behaviour therefore undermines the very immediacy of social relationships that emerge in spontaneous *communitas*.

It is perhaps this normative form of *communitas* that emerged in the streets around London as the week after the Princess of Wales's death wore on. This is because people may have responded spontaneously in the liminal period which immediately followed the princess's death, but the television frame of ritual which evolved out of the initial frame of disaster may have quickly established an appropriate set of procedures. Public participation therefore became more structured and organised, thus undermining the spontaneous and intense connections which people may have felt in the early hours, or even perhaps in the first day or two, after Diana died. At the same time, where normative *communitas* arises or is sustained, there will inevitably be conflict with prevailing structures and ideologies (ibid.). It was therefore this sustained outburst of apparent public feeling that was perceived to be so revolutionary, so contrary to expected models of behaviour and hence so threatening.

Summary

Television schedules in the week between the accident and funeral more or less returned to normal, but the princess's death and its consequences continued to dominate the news output. The news emphasised crisis and conflict, with the apparent public displays of grief being framed as abnormal and the royal family coming under fire for their apparent insensitivity to the public mood. A majority of Tracking Study respondents themselves became increasingly unhappy with the coverage, either for the way it dominated the news or because of its tone. Nonetheless, a quarter of respondents admitted that they viewed the princess in a more sympathetic light after being exposed to some of the tributes.

Most respondents did not participate in the public displays of grief. Those who did participate tended to do so locally, rather than making special trips to London where most of the media attention was focused. The majority of respondents who did participate denied that television had influenced their actions. It is therefore likely that the actual modes of public participation were predicated on increasingly prevalent funerary rituals and on public responses to major disasters. However, 10 per cent of *all* respondents claimed that seeing pictures of crowds in London *did* make them want to take part in some way, irrespective of whether or not they did take part and also irrespective of whether or not the princess's death had personally affected them. This perhaps suggests that they wanted to participate in a particular social experience which the social anthropologist Victor Turner has described as *communitas* (1969).

The high incidence of non-participation combined with the fact that half of BFI respondents were not personally affected by the princess's death suggest that the public grief was not as widespread as depicted. Yet the media frame of disaster tends to emphasise and inflate crisis by focusing on extremes of behaviour which are then deemed to be representative of wider public responses. In the week following the princess's death, this created what Bourdieu has described as a 'reality effect' (1998), where many respondents at home appeared to be convinced of the truth of the media rhetoric that Britain was united in grief. Some referred to the events they were witnessing as 'mass hysteria' or 'Diana-mania'. Others felt concerned or disturbed by the coverage, drawing parallels with totalitarian mass rallies. Many felt the media was responsible for 'whipping it up'.

In a complex crossover between media and social processes, the construction of public grief was also complemented by the media frame which constructed, legitimised and emphasised an arena for ritual performance and transformation. At sites of mourning which had evolved or been constructed as sacred spaces, tourists, visitors, locals and mourners alike were transformed into participants in a collective ritual experience. These people were transformed not just for television and press cameras, but also for themselves and for other participants. Depictions of public grieving therefore became prescriptive and normative.

Notes

1. 'Tragedy impacts on all areas of output', *Ariel*, 9 September 1997, p. 12.
2. Two years later, a French judge recommended that the photographers arrested should not be prosecuted. Martyn Gregory,

'Chase for justice', *The Guardian*, 6 September 1999, p. 6 (Media section).

3. Members of the public had been quoted in the media stating that the Royal Standard should be flown at half-mast out of respect for the dead princess. This was initially refused because protocol determined that the Royal Standard never be lowered to half-mast, even for the death of a King or Queen, because it symbolised the endurance of the institution of the monarchy itself.

4. Nick Higham, 'Change in the air', *Ariel*, 9 September 1997, p. 7.

5. Bernard was an infamous, hard-drinking columnist who died the same week as Diana.

6. Media events, as defined by Dayan and Katz, are pre-planned and advertised. Their analysis of media events will be given extended discussion in the next chapter.

4
The Funeral

The funeral of the Princess of Wales on Saturday 6 September 1997 was a highly complex and symbolically charged event. It came at the end of a week characterised by high 'public' emotion and intense media activity, in which the frame of disaster, despite a rhetoric of unity, had emphasised crisis, disruption and conflict. It involved public attendance in the streets of London, and the participation of royalty and other public figures in a funerary rite for a well-known individual who had died in tragic circumstances. There was a live television relay of images and commentary across the country and around the world. At its peak, during the service at Westminster Abbey, around 32 million people in the United Kingdom watched it live.

Understanding audience responses to the television coverage of this event is no less complex. Around 70 per cent of BFI respondents watched the funeral live. That is to say, they watched the actual funeral service and at least a portion of the procession to Westminster Abbey and the onward drive to Althorp. This means that a higher percentage of respondents watched the funeral compared to the UK population as a whole. While 32 million viewers across the country constitutes an extremely large audience, it only accounts for 56 per cent of the population.[1]

The higher percentage of Tracking Study viewers who watched the funeral may be accounted for by a number of factors. From the outset, we have known that the BFI sample, with its bias towards older, more middle-class respondents, does not constitute an accurate demographic representation of the wider UK public. These respondents, by choosing to participate in the original ODILOT project back in 1988, may have a particular predilection or interest in watching television generally. Older viewers also watch more television than other age groups (Midwinter, 1991) and it is also possible that such viewers are more likely to be interested in televised royal events and to remember previous ones. Nonetheless, this high number of Tracking Study viewers also disguises an intricate and perhaps contradictory range of processes and factors.

The high percentage of BFI respondents who watched the funeral includes people who had not been personally affected by the princess's death. It also includes some people who had participated in the public displays of grief and others who had not. It hides a range of motivations, behaviours and responses in front of the television set. While some who had been affected by the princess's death tuned in and out to parts of the funeral service depending on what they wanted to see, others who had not been previously affected found themselves gripped and moved by the coverage. Some of these previously unaffected even felt tearful. Of those who did not watch the funeral, a third of these claimed to avoid the coverage specifically, having no interest in either Diana or the event. The remainder of non-viewers had previous commitments, with some on holiday and others at work.

Given the range of complicating factors and the complexity of the televised coverage of the funeral and audience responses to it, it is likely that any analysis here will fall far short of a total understanding of the event, if any such understanding is possible. This chapter instead proposes a number of perspectives from which to view the coverage of the Princess of Wales's funeral and assesses their usefulness and limitations. Starting with an examination of Dayan and Katz's sophisticated and wide-ranging accounts of *media events* (1992, 1995), it will look at theories that see such events as functioning to overcome crisis and celebrate social group values. It will then examine how actual audience behaviour might undermine these functions and theories. The way in which the textual properties of the televised coverage may establish analogous relationships with other television and media texts, and how this might elicit certain audience responses, is explored next. The logical (and potentially controversial) conclusions of such an approach and how this may ultimately conflict with and contradict the central premises of the actual live event itself are examined. The chapter concludes with an exploration of the ambiguous nature of this event and its mediation, and suggests that this very ambiguity may be central to the range of audience experiences and behaviours.

Media Events, Conflict Resolution and Celebration of the Social?

For the most part, the Princess of Wales's funeral conforms to Dayan and Katz's account of *media events* (1992, 1995). Media events are televised occasions that are based on interruption and proclaim 'time-out' from routine broadcast schedules. They are monopolistic, dominating the television output for extensive periods across channels and they are broadcast live. These occasions can include major sporting events such as the Olympic Games, major historic events such as moon landings, or major ceremonial occasions such as funerals for people such as J. F. Kennedy (1953) and Winston Churchill (1965). Unlike 'disaster marathons' which mark the traumatic disruption of everyday broadcasting, and which characterised the television output the previous Sunday, media events such as the princess's funeral are pre-planned and publicised, even if 'hastily improvised in the midst of trauma' (Dayan and Katz, 1995, p. 172). They are also broadcast to very large audiences.

In these terms, the funeral of the Princess of Wales was a media event *par excellence*. As an extraordinary intervention in the normal broadcast schedule, it was televised live across four out of the five UK terrestrial channels.[2] It dominated the day's output, with live coverage commencing just after 9 a.m., as the funeral cortège, consisting of a horsedrawn gun carriage bearing the princess's coffin and a small escort of guardsmen and mounted policemen, left Kensington Palace in west London. The coverage followed the cortège along its almost two-hour journey through streets lined with people to Westminster Abbey. At the abbey, from 11 a.m., the coverage continued through the hour-long service marked by hymns, prayers and readings. It included an address by Earl Spencer, the princess's brother, and a live rendition of the song 'Candle in the Wind', especially rewritten for the occasion and sung by Elton John. The service closed with the Archbishop of Canterbury giving the blessing and commendation, followed by a one-minute silence which the public were invited to observe. After the service, BBC 1 and ITV continued to follow the hearse bearing the princess's coffin on its long journey to Althorp in Northamptonshire, where the princess was finally buried, away from the public gaze, after a private family service in the late afternoon. The funeral continued to dominate the news bulletins later in the day and both BBC 1 and ITV showed edited highlights of the day's events in the evening. It attracted an enormous audience in the United Kingdom and abroad.

What makes Dayan and Katz's media event model even more compelling is that they argue that such occasions constitute a celebration of shared values and that events such as the princess's funeral in particular are *designed* to mitigate trauma, alleviate discontinuity and bring closure to periods of disruption (1992; 1995). Of course, communal values can only be celebrated if conflict is first or simultaneously resolved. Organised by agencies external to the broadcast institutions, such events constitute an establishment response to crisis; they act as 'shock absorbers' to contain damage (ibid.). This idea has particular appeal, as the funeral came at the end of a week in which disruption, crisis and conflict appeared to be endemic. As we have seen previously, half of BFI respondents claimed to be personally affected by the princess's death, and the death of someone who is (perceived to be) close can potentially lead to existential crisis and a loss of confidence in the beliefs, practices and patterns of everyday life. As we have also seen, the media frame of disaster highlighted conflict between different groups and the displays of apparent public mourning were framed as abnormal behaviour. With some people upset by the princess's death and others not, tension was also recorded in some households.

The media event model also has close parallels with two other possible perspectives on the event, both of which support the idea that the princess's funeral served to resolve conflict and celebrate group values. The first is perhaps the more standard sociological view of funerals. This is that funerary rites allow the survivors to come to terms with their loss and their new status without the deceased person, and to dispose of the body that symbolises the chaotic and disruptive potency of death (Richardson, 1999). Such rites mark both emotional and symbolic closure. Furthermore, funerary rites function as a celebration of group *survival* (Walter, 1999b). Someone may have died, but funerals ensure that the social group can survive and transcend individual mortality.

The second way we can consider the princess's funeral is as a ceremonial mechanism to bring to an end or to halt the spread of conflict and dispute within the community. Following Turner's discussion of *social dramas*, periods of crisis and liminality are triggered by an infraction of social rules or traumatic disruption of the social fabric (Turner, 1982). At such times, social relations are fractured. This was clearly evident in the wake of the princess's death, as criticism of the cause of the accident abounded and the displays of 'public' grieving were seen as transgressing prescribed codes for bereavement on one level and a dangerous example of 'people power' at another. Ceremonial mechanisms therefore function to bring periods of dispute to a close, with a reintegration of fractious groups or a formal recognition of schism within the community.

In a sense, the model of media events can accommodate such views of funerary rites and social dramas because, as Dayan and Katz argue (1992, 1995), the media unproblematically upholds the definition of an event as proposed by the event's organisers. In this regard, at the heart of the princess's funeral coverage was a funerary ritual which television could not fail to convey with all the emotional, religious and social significance that this entailed. At the same time, the event was also designed to be public, conciliatory and inclusive. The procession in the streets to Westminster Abbey was deemed for public consumption (Davies, 1999), with the route extended to accommodate more spectators. The lowering of the Royal Standard at

Buckingham Palace as the funeral cortège passed was a concession to public demand and intended to signify that the royal family was not out of touch with public sentiment. The service itself was deliberately inclusive with an integrated mix of the traditional and the novel, a blend of Anglican format, royal protocol, contemporary funerary practice and popular appeal (Davies, 1999).

Yet the television coverage of such live events is not just a matter of simple diffusion. In Dayan and Katz's model, media events offer all viewers free and equal access to the whole event. With the princess's funeral, this meant that audiences at home *could*, in theory, watch the event from beginning to end – the procession, the service and the drive to Althorp. Complemented by voice-over commentary explaining the significance of the symbols, songs and rites, viewers were provided with a clearer exposition of the event. Thus, 'The television viewer is drawn into the symbolic meaning of the event even more than is the primary audience on the spot.' (Dayan and Katz; 1992; p. 94) The success of these events is therefore determined by audience size and, in events organised by the establishment or state, the ratings are read 'as a confirmation of loyalty, as a reiteration of the social contract between citizens and their leaders' (ibid., p. 139).

The Spatial and Temporal Frame of Ritual

The issue of what proposes an actual resolution of conflict and crisis and what constitutes an actual celebration of social values is profoundly complex. A semiotic analysis of the princess's funeral, unmediated, is itself worthy of extended research and analysis, and this should rightly exercise cultural commentators, sociologists, social anthropologists and historians for years to come. For the purposes of exploring the interaction between social and media processes here and testing the perspectives outlined above, however, it is worth crudely and briefly propounding a way in which the television coverage of the funeral may have proposed or constituted such conflict resolution and group celebration. The way the coverage may have done this is by reiterating the social group (survival) through the articulation of temporal and spatial structures. First, it

constructed a social group synchronically through the frame of ritual and the positioning of participants, spectators and television
viewers around the country as members of what Anderson (1991)
describes as an 'imagined community'. Secondly, it established a
diachronic framework that demonstrates the longevity and
resilience of the social group. This also provides it with an atempo-
ral quality which transcends individual mortality and group conflict,
while at the same time legitimating structures of power and authority. Such an account here is purely suggestive and is in no way to
be considered exhaustive or exclusive.

The *moment* of the princess's funeral marked both the continu-
ation and culmination of aspects of the week's events and media
coverage. In this sense, we will need to rehearse briefly some of the
points outlined in the previous chapter. In spite of the media frame
of disaster which emphasised conflict and disruption, a rhetoric of
national unity was complemented and reinforced by images of
apparent mass mourning at sites associated with royalty. This simultaneously had symbolic significance because royalty in the United
Kingdom has connotations of the sacred which, in a Durkheimian
analysis, represents the totality of society itself. The depictions of
crowds also suggested a form of intense social experience which
Turner calls *communitas* (1969). This *communitas* may have perhaps
been spontaneous at first; as the week wore on, a more normative
kind of *communitas* may have emerged, as media images offered
prescriptions for appropriate public responses and behaviour. The
transformative aspects of the televisual frame of ritual also turned
those in attendance into participants of some kind. London palaces
and gardens were therefore proposed initially as liminal spaces and
then as sacred centres – loci of pilgrimage where the social could be
experienced. In short, the television commentary and the coverage
of the crowds at these spaces of sacred significance during the week
proposed a sense of collective experience. On the day of the funeral,
this collective experience in London was emphatically reiterated
and simultaneously transmitted to distant others throughout the
country and abroad. In Dayan and Katz's thesis, people watching in

their homes at the farthest geographical reaches of society were simultaneously connected to central and sacred symbols.

This simultaneity and the synchronic social group are, in Dayan
and Katz's model, guaranteed by a number of factors. For Dayan
and Katz, media events are based on interruption. They are marked
out as separate from the programming that occupies routine and
everyday broadcast schedules. They constitute 'time-out' from
those schedules and '[a]udiences recognise them as an invitation –
even a command – to stop their daily routines and join in a holiday
experience' (1992, p. 1). The sense of 'holiday' may at first seem
inappropriate here, being more suitable to other types of media
event such as major sporting occasions, but this is something that
we will return to later. What is important to note here is the idea
that people are expected to drop what they are doing and watch a
televised event.

In Dayan and Katz's scheme, the imperative to watch becomes
even more strongly enforced when that event is monopolisitc, dominating the media and the television schedules. It draws attention to
itself as a significant event. In the United Kingdom, this has particular resonance because public service broadcasting, in its structure
and philosophy, carries with it an ideology of 'public' interest and
'public' good. This is particularly the case with the BBC, which automatically confers state, national or establishment status on the rituals
it televises (Bocock, 1974; Cardiff and Scannell, 1987). This was
something that one BFI respondent observed:

> *I watched BBC 1 because I saw this as an 'establishment' event and
> viewed BBC 1 as still being part of the establishment.* (F36)

Most BFI respondents did not specifically identify which channel
they watched, but BARB data seems to support the idea that people
watched the 'establishment' channel because 59 per cent of viewers
who watched the funeral tuned to BBC 1, compared to 36 per cent
who watched it on ITV.[3] If an event is televised live on national television, it is deemed to have national importance and interest, and by

default is expected to attract a 'national' audience. The point here is that everyone is expected or imagined to be watching the event at the same moment. This establishes what Anderson describes as an 'imagined community', where, in even the smallest nation, people do not know each other, but synchronicity in a particular activity, such as reading the morning paper, establishes a co-temporal relationship. Other people are expected to be having a similar experience at exactly the same time.[4]

In some cases, that co-temporal relationship involves physical proximity. As Dayan and Katz (1992) argue, media events overcome the differentiated and fragmented nature of the television audience by giving 'new status' to living rooms. 'Television is revived as the family focus, commanding attention and interest and bringing family members and friends together again' (ibid., p. 195). Loosely translated, the living room is transformed into a public, rather than a private, place. Drawing on the work of Shils and Young (1953), where feuding neighbours were reconciled to the point that one could watch the Queen's coronation on the other's television, Dayan and Katz suggest that people want to watch media events together. Indeed, a handful of BFI respondents described scenes of families watching the television or, in some instances, friends meeting at home specifically to watch the funeral with each other:

> My family and I watched the entire funeral. My husband has his own business, but he was shut for the day as a mark of respect. We did not make any special effort, we just felt it was the appropriate thing to do. At times it was difficult because we have a thirteen-month-old baby and sometimes he got bored, so we took it in turns to entertain him. We watched BBC 1 until she reached her final resting place around 2.15 p.m. We stayed at home in our breakfast room, drinking tea and crying. It did not feel right to go out on such a sad day. (F24)

> A friend held a mourning session, five women and children linked up around 10 a.m., to catch up on each other's reactions to the week's

events, take it in turns with the kids, to cook, to drink and weep together.
There were laughs as well as tears. (F41)

As well as establishing or positing group cohesion in the face of disruption, the television coverage of the funeral also placed the Princess of Wales's death within a diachronic framework that served to emphasise both the historical and the transcendent quality of the social group. It has been observed that many of the rituals involved with the monarchy are of recent origin, especially those relating to the media (Hobsbawm, 1983). They constitute 'invented traditions' which Hobsbawm defines as 'a set of practices, normally governed by overtly or tacitly accepted rules and of a ritual and symbolic nature, which seek to inculcate certain values and norms of behaviour by repetition, which automatically implies continuity with the past' (ibid., p. 1). These are particularly important, he argues, for the notion of the 'nation' and its attendant symbols and ideologies, which are relatively recent phenomena. This is because notions of the 'nation', nationalism and nation state are predicated on innovation and 'social engineering'. What is paradoxical, Hobsbawm asserts, is that while the 'nation' is a modern construct, nations tend to claim:

> ... to be the opposite of novel, namely rooted in the remotest antiquity,
> and the opposite of constructed, namely human communities so 'natural'
> as to require no definition other than self-assertion. (1983, p. 14)

What this means is that 'invented traditions' contribute to a sense of timelessness, a feeling of 'this is how it is and as it always has been'. The institution of the royal Christmas broadcast on radio in 1932, for example, is such an example of an invented tradition which is now a taken-for-granted aspect of the Christmas day television schedule, part of the Christmas ritual. This appeal to antiquity is significant because it legitimates existing social structures, hierarchies and relations of power. It is also significant here because it can affirm and reaffirm the survival and duration of the social group beyond biology and the death of an important individual. Kings and queens may come and go, but 'there will always be an England'.

Television does not only make such invented traditions available to a wider public, but is also intricately interrelated to an anterior and transcendent order through the patterns and conventions of genre. As Dayan and Katz have argued, media events themselves constitute a particular genre of broadcast output. It was therefore the complex interrelationship between tradition and genre which *effectively* elevated the status of the princess's funeral to a 'royal' and 'state' event. Occupying a place on the periphery of the royal family, the Princess of Wales was a constitutionally and symbolically ambiguous figure. As a result, her funeral was not deemed to be a 'state funeral', but, in the words of a Palace official, 'would be a unique event for unique person'. Yet, as the BBC reporter John Simpson stated on the *Nine O'clock News* (1 September 1997), 'It may not technically be a royal funeral, but it will certainly look like one'.

Within the broadcast canon for such events, Simpson was right. Legitimised by live broadcast across most of the British terrestrial television channels, for example, it included all the relevant framing and signifiers of a state event such as royal personnel and the symbolic geography and architecture of state. Following the procession past Buckingham Palace, along the Mall, through Whitehall and past the Houses of Parliament to Westminster Abbey, the television frame captured the sacred spaces where previous historic and royal events had taken place. Even the strategic location of cameras outside the entrance to Westminster Abbey ensured that the television frame was filled with Gothic architecture, implying the old, traditional and sacred, and excluded the neighbouring modern and secular Queen Elizabeth II Conference Centre. Other aspects such as the music also played a significant part in establishing the funeral as part of a broadcast canon of royal events. In particular, one respondent was sadly reminded of the wedding between Diana and Charles in 1981.

Hearing 'I Vow to Thee My Country' took me back to the wedding and made me sad how things worked out. (F37)

Songs such as this and the national anthem, with their connotations of monarchy, God and country, have deep symbolic resonance. Even the commentary was part of the broadcast tradition for such events. As we have seen, Dayan and Katz argue that such commentary draws the television spectator more deeply into the symbolic importance of the event by explaining the relevance and traditions behind certain parts of the ceremony (1992; 1995). At an aesthetic level, however, the voice-over commentary can take on mystical qualities and power. This is because the voice-over narration can represent a 'radical otherness', a voice outside of both time and space creating an impression of permanence and transcendence (Doane, 1985). Interestingly here, a BFI respondent alluded to these processes when he claimed to watch the live funeral on BBC because the commentator, David Dimbleby, was the son of the late broadcaster Richard Dimbleby, who had commentated at the Queen's Coronation in 1953 and at the funeral of Winston Churchill in 1965:

> *The reason for this decision [watching BBC] was the choice of David*
> *Dimbleby to be commentator and particularly by their telling*
> *prospective viewers that David's father Richard had always covered*
> *important national events in the past. From this we gathered we were to*
> *infer that if father made a damn good job of it, so would David.* (M75)

Such signifiers as the royal personnel, the settings, music and commentary all place the funeral in direct lineage to other royal and state events. The princess's death and funeral was therefore part of an age-old story that would continue.

Taking these processes into account, therefore, it is possible to argue that the television coverage of the Princess of Wales's funeral resolved crisis and conflict by positioning participants and viewers alike as part of a geographic and historically imagined community. On one level, it proposed solutions to the kind of existential crisis that the death of someone close provokes. On another, the iteration of collective experience proposed that conflict had been resolved and order restored. In a world turned upside down by death and the suspension of meaningful and hierarchical structures, the television coverage of the princess's funeral re-established, renewed and reassured the individual viewer of his or her place in the world. Viewers were interpellated as meaningful historical or national subjects. It offered symbolic resources for the (re)construction of identities and for a sense of belonging to a meaningful community. Viewers were positioned as part of a transcendent order that was bigger than individual mortality. In the grand scheme of things, as depicted on television, life goes on and it has meaning.

The Problematic Audience

A number of problems emerge here. As we have seen, Dayan and Katz make a number of claims for media events which are compelling in light of the funeral of the Princess of Wales. They argue that people stop what they are doing to watch a televised event and celebrate shared values. Viewers have free and equal access to the whole of the event and they commune with central symbols. Viewership constitutes participation in a collective experience. Fragmentation and distance are overcome to unite the social group. Dayan and Katz describe the experience that the media events generates, after Turner, as *communitas* (1992), a concept which we explored in the last chapter. Furthermore, because television upholds the event as defined by the organisers, viewership constitutes a legitimation of the event. Legitimation, mandate and success are measured by audience size. Dayan and Katz's account, however, is undermined when actual audience behaviours, motivations and interests are considered.

Around 70 per cent of BFI respondents watched the princess's funeral live. Approximately 20 per cent of respondents did not watch due to other commitments or for reasons not specified. A hard core of 10 per cent of respondents, however, said that they had no interest in either Diana or the event, and deliberately avoided the coverage. As also previously observed, the incidence of viewership of the funeral amongst Tracking Study respondents is much higher than across the country as a whole, which was 56 per cent (source: BARB).

The BARB data raises a crude but obvious question. How can it be argued that the princess's funeral was a huge national event of shared communion if fewer than half the population, for whatever reasons, were not watching? Furthermore, the 70 per cent of BFI respondents who watched the funeral cannot be treated unproblematically. This is because this figure inevitably includes people who had not been profoundly upset or affected by the princess's death, people who had been unhappy with the television coverage during the week and people who had been surprised of appalled at the apparent scenes of public outpouring of grief. If viewers included a diverse range of followers and dissenters, to what extent can we ascribe a homogenous range of values and motivational factors? We therefore have to take into account actual audience behaviour in front of their television screens.

One of the characteristics of the princess's funeral was that it was monopolistic; this is undoubtedly one of the reasons that so many Tracking Study respondents watched it on television. Not only did the event dominate the television schedules that Saturday, but also many shops, bars, cafés and businesses had been closed and sports events cancelled as a mark of respect for the dead princess. As a result, many found themselves at home with nothing to do that Saturday morning when they would perhaps normally have been at work, shopping or at a sporting fixture. Interestingly, following her investigation of 'shop window shrines' in Bath, Bowman (1999) suggests that women working in shops would have been a prime demographic for sympathy with the princess, and it was a lot of these people who were at home on the Saturday morning. Nonetheless, for some, the closure of shops and businesses was a problem. This is the case for the following two respondents; while one consequently watched the funeral, the other did not:

> I watched some of the funeral on BBC. (As I had planned to go to the local shops I found it most inconvenient to find they were shut!). (F82)

> I was very reluctant to stop at home on my own in the morning, but

there seemed no alternative as everywhere was closed at least until 2 p.m.
There were no sporting events in the country – all had been postponed
or cancelled. So I decided to carry on with some domestic work in the
home. (M71)

In another instance, a respondent (F24) recorded that she did not
particularly want to watch the funeral, but as she was visiting her 'in-
laws', who were watching, she ultimately had no option. For those
who did watch, not all of them may have done so with the same sense
of gravitas as those who were profoundly upset by the event. Just as
television provides background accompaniment to much household
activity, what Lull describes as an 'environmental source' (1990), the
following respondent shows how life, such as socialising and organ-
ising parties, goes on even when an apparently major national event
is being televised live:

I think I would have slept through the funeral cortège because a friend
was visiting and we spent most of the night talking and drinking, but we
were having a party on the Saturday night and the phone started ringing
very early with people making arrangements and asking for directions. I
saw Earl Spencer's speech – which I thought was very powerful. Soon
after that we discovered Lassie Come Home *on BBC 2. Hurrah!* (F23)

One suspects that this respondent would ordinarily have had on a
popular television chart show or some other Saturday morning
youth-orientated programming that has a cultish following with
some adults if the schedules had not been so dramatically altered.

Although Dayan and Katz argue that living rooms are transformed into 'public' spaces during media events (1992, 1995), and
although we saw that for some BFI respondents this was the case as
they joined together to watch the funeral, other respondents suggest
that this is not always or necessarily so. Some refer to a more fractured space. The following respondent, for example, quoted above
discussing how a 'friend held a mourning session', hints at how this
may have worked:

The male partners elected to be on their own with radio or TV at studios,
sheds or garages nearby. They wept alone. (F41)

What these 'male partners' thought about the event and how they
responded to the televised funeral is a matter of speculation, and it
is unknown here whether they wept or not. Nonetheless, what this
respondent suggests is that some rooms, for the duration of the
funeral at least, became gendered spaces. This is significant because
the issue of gender may have determined whether or not some viewers had 'free and equal access' to the whole televised event, the
functional equivalent of a 'festive experience', as Dayan and Katz
suggest (1992). This is because the contingent and situated nature of
reception can affect that experience. Some may simply be too busy
to pay close attention to the coverage in its entirety:

I switched on the TV and occasionally went in to see what was
happening, but basically I was scrubbing the kitchen floor for most of it.
(F37)

I watched alone (daughter in bed with flu, husband wasn't having
anything to do with it!) while doing my very necessary housework. (F45)

Despite their housework, it is conceivable that these respondents
still followed the funeral closely. This is because it has been suggested
that women develop ways of half-watching and half-listening to
favourite television programmes while engaged in a variety of hectic and frantic household tasks such as cooking and looking after
children (Hobson, 1982). What this does suggest, however, is that
some people did *not* drop what they were doing to watch the funeral
or, importantly in the case of women, who spend more of their time
engaged in household chores than men,[5] perhaps *could not* drop
their other activities. The construction of gendered space and the
ability to view were also referred to by a handful of other female
respondents, but for perhaps slightly different reasons, as the following two testify:

Although I intended to watch the actual service, I spent all day watching. I had no intention of watching it continually, but, as a number of friends have agreed, it was impossible to pull away. I tried to watch alone as I felt unable to grieve in the company of my family, so I watched in whichever room had no one present. (F40)

I was not planning to watch the funeral, but on waking up I switched on the TV and found I could not stop watching. I watched BBC 1, mostly alone, with my mother joining me for the service itself. We watched in the kitchen, as it did not seem as 'settled' as watching in the living room (we could pretend we were on our way to do other things!). (F24)

Leaving aside the compulsive aspects of the funeral coverage, which we will return to later, these respondents appear to describe feelings of discomfort at watching the funeral. There may be a number of reasons for this, some to do with the princess's death and some perhaps to do with everyday attitudes towards television and viewing behaviours. One possible reason relates to the tension and conflict in some homes in the week following the princess's death.

Some respondents were critical of the television coverage devoted to the princess's death and others expressed surprise or distaste at the apparent scenes of public grieving. Some viewers, especially those who had been affected by Diana's death, may have therefore wanted to watch the funeral away from other household members who had been critical or who may have potentially been less than reverential in front of the television screen. Another related reason, concerned with more stiff-upper-lip attitudes towards grief or prescribed bereavement behaviour, is that some may have wanted to keep their feelings private, to respond openly and emotionally out of view of other people without embarrassment or censure.

Another reason may be found in connection with everyday viewing. This is because it has been argued that women often take guilty pleasure in watching certain kinds of romantic or sentimental programming (Morley, 1986) or videos (Gray, 1987, 1992). Both Morley and Gray found that women prefer to watch these programmes or films with female friends or by themselves because their viewing preferences are considered to come at the bottom of family or household hierarchies of taste. In these hierarchies, men are deemed to like factual programmes or 'realistic' fiction (Morley) or action (Gray). Women may therefore be embarrassed or apologetic about their own preferences for romantic stories or 'weepies'. Anticipated or actual viewing of the funeral by some women may therefore have been equated on some level with the guilty pleasure of watching such romantic stories and they therefore wanted to watch either alone or with other women, but in any event away from men. What complicates matters here is that Gauntlett and Hill found that there was some elision between male and female tastes amongst Tracking Study respondents (1999). Some men were keen viewers of soap operas and some women avid watchers of news and current affairs programmes. Furthermore, as we have found here, men, too, were personally affected by the princess's death and, as we will see later, some were moved by the funeral. Yet, for what is inevitably a complex mix of the kinds of reasons outlined above, it was only female respondents who referred to this kind of discomfort watching with other people – although this does not necessarily rule out the possibility the some men did not feel the same way.

It is clear that a number of problems have emerged here. First, despite the very large size of the UK audience, it is clear that a lot of people were *not* watching. Secondly, for those who did watch, not all of them necessarily wanted to or were able to give it their full and serious attention. Of course, not everyone was distressed by the princess's death, and this may account for the apparent nonchalance of some viewers. Thirdly, the nature of the event meant that the living room was not necessarily transformed into public and collective space. Issues of grief, gender or conflict may have made this problematic. Audience fragmentation may also have been sustained by the prevalence of multiple television sets; people could watch around the house, with whom they wanted to, in a way not available to viewers in single-set households at the time of the Queen's coronation or the funerals of J. F. Kennedy and Winston Churchill. What these points mean is that not everyone dropped what they were doing to watch an event which, in Dayan and Katz's terms, celebrated shared values. Not everyone had equal access to the televised coverage and therefore, by extension, they did not have 'free and equal access' to the entire funeral.

Such audience responses and behaviour highlight the mediated experience of the princess's funeral. It is this mediation which ultimately, and self-evidently, separates media events from non-mediated funerary rituals or ceremonial mechanisms for resolving social dramas. This is significant because it means that watching an event such as the Princess of Wales's funeral on television is a very different experience to physical presence, participation and unmediated spectatorship of a ritual or ceremony. As we saw in the last chapter, and in contradiction to Dayan and Katz, the mediation of television is disruptive to the experience of *communitas*. To briefly summarise, *space–time distanciation* as explored by Thompson (1990) means that symbolic forms are taken out of one context and transmitted into another. As Thompson goes on to argue, this intermediation is also monologic, a one-way process. In just the same way that people feel they know media personalities well, through non-reciprocal intimacy at a distance (Thompson 1995), so, too, is the viewer engaged in a non-reciprocal relationship with an event and the participants and spectators at that event. Watching television, or engaging in any other form of media consumption involving distant others, absolves viewers of any responsibility to behave or act in a certain way. They do not have to offer any commitment in return in this one-way relationship.

What this suggests is that the act of watching television is not *performative*. Free from the surveillance of other spectators or participants, viewers do not have to behave in prescribed ways. People *can* organise parties, laugh and joke, make breakfast or chat their way through the service. Of course, this does not mean to say that members of the public who lined the streets for the princess's funeral cortège did not laugh or talk. The difference, however, is that actual physical presence can entail a moment of transformation where the spectator or tourist becomes an actual participant – for the actual person, for other people in attendance watching the event, for the principal actors involved in the main ritual and for those watching at home. As social anthropologists such as Watson (1988) have often argued, actual spectatorship of ritual is crucial to the event's correct performance and efficacy. It ensures participant orthopraxy on the one hand and legitimation on the other. It means that spectators become participants because they can heckle or physically intervene if they feel that the rite is not being performed properly. It also means that they can validate correct or pleasing per-formance. In the case of the princess's funeral, watching at home precluded the possibility of physical intervention, either by voicing disapproval or, as was the case, by applauding Earl Spencer's speech or throwing flowers at the coffin and hearse.

As a result, as in Ellis's formulation, the television experience is one of non-involvement, isolation and insulation from the given event (1982). Mediation by broadcast institutions and the techno-logical apparatus of television impose intervening processes and structures between producers and receivers, and this inhibits the experience of *communitas* which can only exist where there is an absence of structure (Turner, 1969).

The Melodramatic Closure?
Another way to look at the Princess of Wales's funeral is in terms of media narrative. There are a number of reasons why this should be considered. First, the variety of audience reactions outlined above demonstrate that viewership of media events does not necessarily constitute participation in a collective ritual. Some of the respon-dents watched the coverage avidly, some had it on in the background, and others dropped in and out in the same way that they might any other television text or narrative. Secondly, by being mediated, the funeral coverage was conveyed in a media register. It told a story and was part of a bigger story. This becomes even more compelling when you consider Dayan and Katz's argument that media events are 'translated' into a fictional register which has much in common with

fiction films (1992), as we shall explore below. Thirdly, when she was alive, Diana's life could be understood in relation to four different types of narrative: the fairy tale, the classic narrative, the soap opera narrative and news (Geraghty, 1998). When she was alive, Geraghty argued, the soap opera narrative was the most appropriate perspective from which to consider the media coverage of her life because it was continuous and open-ended. As we have argued, the princess's life had parallels with the melodramatic ups and downs of such soaps. The media narrative of Diana's life was, however, radically subverted when she died.

A consideration of the television coverage of the funeral in terms of media narrative also has some benefits. It might allow us to look at how television provided some kind of closure to the week's events. It might help us understand how it may have helped people come to terms with the princess's death and the loss of someone close. Finally, it might help us understand why some of those who had not previously been upset by the princess's death found the funeral compelling or moving.

Dayan and Katz suggest that media events are broadcast in a 'fictional register' (1992). This is because these events are predicated on aesthetics of realism characteristic, and inherited from, they argue, 'classical' Hollywood cinema. As they suggest: 'The conferral of media-event status on a given occasion consists in pulling it away from the news and translating it in a fictional register. The result is a text which neutralizes the opposition between fiction and news.' (1992, p. 114). What is crucial here is that media events are different from the news. Whereas news stresses conflict and disruption, media events, as previously described, stress resolution and community. Dayan and Katz go on to argue that, whereas the viewer is invited *into* the media event, news coverage distances the viewer. As discussed in Chapter 1, for example, television newsreaders ordinarily act as a barrier between viewers and unsettling and disturbing news reports (Morse, 1986). What is significant about the news is the way in which it juxtaposes face-to-camera presentation with cutaway segments, filmed reports and interviews within a short time frame, potentially creating an alienating effect and alerting the viewer to the constructed nature of the televisual text.

The difference with media events, argue Dayan and Katz, is that they utilise aesthetics of realism inherited from classical Hollywood cinema. MacCabe (1974) has elsewhere described these as 'classic realist texts' (1974), in which the organisation of editing elides the constructed nature of the text to create an illusion of unmediated reality. In film, for example, temporality, space, editing and point of view are subordinated to cause-and-effect chains to create a natural and coherent 'objective story reality' against which the action is fore-grounded (Bordwell and Thompson, 1993). In media events, temporal and spatial sequences are related in a similarly continuous manner. The 'coherence of the broadcast derives from the pro-gression of the event itself, a characteristic of fiction made all the more salient by the fact that the event is broadcast live' (Dayan and Katz, 1992, p. 115).

Like fiction films, therefore, media events 'allow their spectators to follow the event from within' (ibid.). Dayan and Katz go on to sug-gest that 'spectators are invited to inhabit the event through the mediation of the primary audience in attendance, to see through the eyes of those directly involved' (ibid.). On one level, this may be problematic because viewers watching on television see more than the 'primary audience' actually at the scene of the event. As Ellis has observed, the delegation of looking to another party ultimately serves to distance the viewer from what is depicted on screen. It may therefore be more useful here to adapt, or perhaps simply reword, Dayan and Katz's argument to suggest instead that viewers see through the eyes of the principal participants. This is significant because another aspect of the fictional register which Dayan and Katz identify is the tension established by indices that 'point towards private feelings or emotion' (ibid.). It is in this way, Dayan and Katz argue, that the viewers take part in the action from within. They understand the psychological motivations of characters and identify with them. In this sense, people watching the princess's funeral may have identified with the survivors and their grief. It was perhaps because of processes such as these that some respondents, like the following one who had previously been unaffected, found themselves engaging with the funeral coverage:

> *I had not intended to watch all day – nor did my husband mean to watch at all but we found that we were drawn into this sad story and were touched that this woman should be taken so soon, unloved and unsupported as she was by the Royals.* (F77)

If the funeral of the Princess of Wales is to be considered in terms of filmic narrative, the most appropriate narrative format here would undoubtedly be the melodrama. As we saw in Chapter 2, Diana, in life, could have been perceived as a melodramatic heroine – the ups and downs of her life could be seen in a melodramatic light.

Interestingly, there were three particular aspects of the princess's funeral which were recalled most frequently by Tracking Study respondents, and these could each potentially be read as shorthand reminders of the melodramatic nature of Diana's life and death. These were the song 'Candle in the Wind' written and sung live by Elton John, Earl Spencer's speech in the funeral service, and the wreath on the princess's coffin with a card inscribed with the word 'Mummy':

> *Throughout the day I found myself crying – especially at Elton John's song and cheering at Earl Spencer's speech.* (F32)

> *... the one part which stood out was Elton John's song – this was the only bit which made both my mother and myself cry as he sang it with so much emotion.* (F27)

As Williamson noted in relation to Prince William and Prince Harry, 'The thought of two children with no mother and a lifetime of public duty was – and is – bleakly poignant. It would be a hard-hearted person who could remain untouched by that card that read, simply, "Mummy"' (1998, p. 26). Indeed, the following respondent who had previously been dismissive about the event, a former soldier who had seen active service and who had been angered that so much attention be given to one person, was disarmingly open and honest:

> *OK – so I've proved what an insensitive and heartless old chauvinist I am. Well, I AM – which makes it rather painful for me to confess that I completely broke down into sobbing when TV showed a small bunch of flowers on the coffin, bearing the single word 'Mummy'. That was heartbreaking.* (M45)

While the speech and the song are reminders of the struggles and vicissitudes of Diana's life and that happiness had been snatched away from her, the inscription 'Mummy' may also have had more profound melodramatic connotations. In his discussion of the melodramatic film format, Steve Neale explores the ability of classic 'Hollywood' melodrama to move its spectators to tears. What he argues is that melodramas are marked by chance happening, coincidences, surprises, '*deus ex machina* endings'. Like Ang's discussion of the excessive plot structure in *Dallas*, Neale argues that, in the Hollywood 'tear-jerker', there is 'an excess of effects over cause, of the extraordinary over the ordinary. Hence the emergence of terms like fate, chance and destiny' (1986, pp. 6–7). Often the protagonist, struggling against social norms, rules or circumstances beyond their control, is just a hair's breadth away from happiness. Often that happiness is denied at the last moment, just as Diana died when she had apparently found happiness in love. As a result, 'Tears are the product of powerlessness. They presume two mutually opposed facts: [t]hat it is clear how the present state of things should be changed – and that this change is impossible' (ibid., p. 8).

What seems remarkably apposite about Neale's analysis here is that he suggests that part of the emotional impact of this genre of film is that '[m]elodrama is full of characters who wished to be loved, who are worthy of love, and whom the spectator therefore wishes to be loved' (ibid., p. 17). The princess's funeral, and the apparent public mourning during the week, may have served to emphasise that

Diana had been apparently loved by millions, and that tragically she never realised this. Neale's analysis, drawing on psychoanalytic theory, appears even more compelling when he argues that spectators want such characters to be loved because it lies 'in a nostalgic fantasy of childhood characterised by union with the mother: a state of total love ...' (ibid., p. 17). As Neale goes on to argue:

> As in infancy, crying here emerges precisely at the point of realisation of the loss of the union of the mother and child. It serves to mark and articulate the absence of the mother and the wish for her to return, for a state of being prior to this. (ibid., p. 19)

If we accept such an analysis, then the identification with the two princes left behind who have lost their mother had a doubly powerful resonance.

Taking into account the standardised 'cause-and-effect' chain of 'realist' Hollywood narratives, the invitation to follow the event from within, the melodramatic reminders, the denial of love and happiness, and the loss of the mother, the filmic register has one other emotionally potent characteristic which differentiates it from television genres such as soap opera and news – closure. Films are hermetically sealed. Once they have ended they are over. It is perhaps in this way that the funeral coverage, in a melodramatic film register, brought about a final and irrevocable closure. The princess was dead and the spatial separation and sequestration of her body from society was irreversible.

Thus, the climax of the television coverage was the long journey of the hearse containing Diana's body from Westminster Abbey to Althorp, where she was to be buried, after a private ceremony, on an island in private ground away from the public gaze. As Richardson suggests, the body is a great symbol of the potency of death, (1999), thus the body must be disposed of and separated from society where it can no longer present a threat to the stable ontological structures and routine operations of everyday life. Described by Richardson as a 'lonely journey', this coverage had all the pathos and emotional power of a hero or heroine walking into the sunset at the end of a movie. The princess, whose popularity had been witnessed in a groundswell of apparent public grief on her death, was to be consigned to a lonely grave. This provided the climactic punctuation (an exclamation mark!) to the final frame of the drama, conflict and emotion of the week.

Sad Stories or Roman Holidays?

If we consider that aspects of the television coverage of the funeral were melodramatic, or at least analogous to certain melodramatic narratives, we have to consider the possibility that some members of the public might actually have *enjoyed* or derived some degree of *entertainment* from this event. One respondent, appalled by the media overkill and the apparent 'public' grieving, explicitly referred to this possibility:

> *Close-ups of the crowds, kids grinning and waving at the camera and a burst of applause as the black cars left ... It all struck me as sickening. I couldn't help thinking, 'It's a Roman holiday.'*[6] (M63)

This is, however, a particularly tricky issue to examine in that few people would readily admit to 'enjoyment' of death and destruction, and certainly in the case of Diana none of the BFI respondents did. Part of the problem is that such feelings are probably confusing, hard to articulate and, even if understood or recognised, probably appear quite tasteless to acknowledge or disclose. So, while no one claimed to find the coverage over the week 'entertaining', some respondents did admit to feelings of confusion and guilt, as the following viewer (F45) suggested: 'The saturation coverage was a trifle ghoulish, but then I didn't switch off.' Another viewer (F37), who complained about television hypocrisy at criticising the tabloid press, went on to add, 'Yet I was glued to it just the same.'

What is evident, however, is that the combination of emotion, conflict and dramatic intrigue on television could hardly have failed to complicate any feelings experienced by the viewer at home. Nonetheless, the funeral coverage had a different quality to the news output over the previous week. As we have seen in this chapter, media events are deliberately meant to be restorative, collective, celebratory and a 'time-out' from normal television. Sharing in common elements of Hollywood weepies, there may have been components of the television coverage which viewers found gratifying, as the following respondents allude:

I 'enjoyed' the funeral ... I sang the hymns and wept buckets. (F44)

Another very sad and tearful yet beautiful and unreal day. (F48)

The point here is that, simply put, people *do* enjoy sad films or sad songs. Yet there might also be something morbidly compelling or fascinating about the princess's death and funeral, as these two respondents suggest:

I found the whole thing grimly fascinating and riveting in an odd sort of way though there can be few things less interesting than watching a funeral procession at such length. (F36)

Both of us found it compelling viewing. We'd only intended to watch the funeral service but stayed watching until the motorcade was well on the motorway. (F48)

What is particular about the week's news output and the funeral coverage is that it was very different to everyday broadcasting and, using the term suggested by Mellencamp (1990), it was *deathly*. The repetitive broadcast output has the ability to promote secure and stable ontological structures on a daily basis, almost to the point of banality. Yet at an ideological level, Doane argues that 'catastrophic events' actually deny the process that television is a banal and commercial enterprise, that a catastrophic event 'corroborates television's access to the momentary, the discontinuous and the real' (Doane, 1990, p. 238). As Bourdieu has argued, for example, television news, for professional and commercial reasons, is not allowed to be boring. Television journalists actually seek the sensational and the spectacular; they search for the extraordinary and the exceptional – in newspaper parlance, they look for the 'scoop'. To this end, television (and other forms of journalism) actually promotes conflict and drama:

> Television calls for dramatization, in both senses of the term: it puts an event on stage, puts it in images. In doing so, it exaggerates the importance of that event, its seriousness, and its dramatic, even tragic character. (Bourdieu, 1998, p. 19).

In this sense, the extraordinary, extensive, emotive and emphatic television coverage on Sunday 31 August and Saturday 6 September, and the days in between, was indeed a break from the usual dull and banal broadcast output. Something interesting was happening – it was something to talk about, an opportunity to explore emotions not normally experienced. In what John Langer refers to as the 'falling chimney syndrome', he suggests, after Susan Sontag (1974, p. 425), that people enjoy the 'aesthetics of destruction'. Watching mediated events releases spectators from their normal obligations and responsibilities, and they can derive a perverse enjoyment of the suffering of others (Langer, 1998). Such enjoyment, Langer suggests, is 'organized around the complementary positions of the Ludic and the Luddite' (ibid., p. 157) and allows people to explore or play, and to create new experiences and understandings of the world.

In a world in which death has become increasingly sequestrated into institutions such as hospitals and residential homes for the elderly (Ariès, 1976), perhaps one of the few ways in which people can experience death is through the media. So in just the same way that some people enjoy watching horror movies or violence on television, the feelings of anxiety that are aroused by the depiction of 'catastrophe' might in some way be pleasurable (Mellencamp, 1990). As Liebes suggests in discussion of disaster marathons, the scenes of destruction, the bloody violence and raw emotion have an almost 'visceral' quality. Such coverage can cater 'to the voyeuristic, even pornographic aspects of viewing' (1998, p. 77). Indeed, comparing the death of Diana in a car accident to David Cronenberg's controversial film *Crash* (1996), adapted from J. G. Ballard's novel where people elicit sexual arousal from re-creating car crashes where celebrities die, Winston Wheeler Dixon argues that there is a vogue in contemporary Hollywood cinema for disaster and spectacle (1999). This is an extension, he argues, of a trend in various types of modern art – of which he exemplifies the series of pictures that Andy Warhol created in the 1960s looking at car crashes – which serve as a denial of death. It has been suggested that part of this fascination is that it is life affirming, the sense of 'That's not me' (Doane, 1990).

Yet such responses are not just exclusive to television. It has been noted, for example, that people will often congregate at the scene of disasters and watch (Cathcart, 1997). Cathcart also suggests, after Raphael (1986), that 'rather than being morbid or voyeuristic, in this way people attempt to master their fear of death and affirm the vigour of their own life' (ibid., p. 504).

Ambiguity and the Quasi-Liminal

That the Princess of Wales's funeral may have provided some kind of televisual entertainment is of course unsettling and some may find this position too extreme. After all, this was not a media fiction or a melodramatic film. It was the live coverage of an actual funerary rite for someone who had actually died, an event which inevitably caused distress to her friends and family, and which seemed personally to affect people who felt they had known her through her media exposure. A totally textual or entertainment-based model is therefore far from adequate in understanding the funeral coverage. At the same time, neither is the media event model totally satisfactory for understanding the event and its impacts. It did not necessarily constitute a shared ritual or celebration of group values, not everyone 'was in it together', and it did not constitute an experience of *communitas* in the way that Dayan and Katz believe such events should. What makes the princess's funeral so complex is the involvement of different groups and different symbolic forms.

First, there is the actual ceremony or ritual itself. With parallels to text–audience debates which argue over whether texts are deterministic or audiences resistant, social anthropologists have long argued over whether rituals have the potential to sustain the status quo or to be subversive. In this debate, rituals have become regarded as fields in which competing identity, status and power claims and conferrals can be contested. Rituals, like texts, can be read in a number of different ways, both by participants and by spectators.

This becomes even more complicated when spectators come to be considered as participants themselves. Their actual presence, critical intervention or validation can undermine or legitimise correct or appropriate performance. During the princess's funeral service at Westminster Abbey, for example, members of the public outside and in Hyde Park watching on giant screens applauded Earl Spencer's speech explicitly criticising the media and implicitly criticising the royal family. Such applause could potentially be read as subversive to the conciliatory aims of the funeral event. Yet, heard inside the abbey, the applause was taken up by members of the congregation. As a result, '[t]he sound of clapping united those inside and outside the Abbey' (Davies, 1999). It could therefore be argued that the response to the Earl's speech was reconciliatory because it marked consensus. The complex elision between spectatorship and participation was also demonstrated in the previous chapter when we argued that people attended London sites during the week with different intentions and motivations. Those people who turned up to look at the flowers were themselves transformed into mourners, while those who turned up to lay flowers or sign a condolence book also became tourists.

Secondly, there is the live transmission of this event. This inevitably involves some degree of distortion, refraction or interference through the institutional mechanisms, broadcast aesthetics, logistical requirements and technological apparatus of the television medium. As Becker has argued, for example, the media plays a crucial role in constituting public events as ritual. Not only does it set apart such events from everyday life, as it did with the disruption of the normal Saturday schedules, but also it contributes to the internal structure of the ritual through the selection and transmission of particular aspects of the event (Becker, 1995, 1998). This has parallels with Dayan and Katz's assertion that television viewers have access – by watching the whole event and through commentaries which explain the significance of certain symbols, traditions or performances – to a deeper understanding of the event's meaning than those actually in attendance. This means that what is portrayed to viewers by television is necessarily different to what would be witnessed or experienced by those at the scene. This means also that people may have different responses to the television coverage to those at the scene. Not only might they have different responses to the central ritual performance, but they might also have different responses to the representation of the spectators. In one example, a respondent thought the clapping at the funeral was 'a bit weird', while another might have been more concerned about safe driving on the hearse's journey through the streets of north London to the motorway:

> *When people threw flowers on the windscreen of the car, I was trying to figure out how long it would be before they would have to be moved off.*
> (F16)

In just in the same way that ritual can be read differently, so, too, can television texts. The voice-over commentaries and depiction of certain images and performance may serve to privilege or overdetermine certain symbols and meanings, but television audiences, too, can be resistant and make their own readings.

Thirdly, as we have already seen in this chapter, people can also *behave* differently in front of their television sets to people attending the event. Watched in private, people's viewing behaviours are not monitored or prescribed in the same way that they would be in public. This, too, suggests that viewing the funeral on television is a different order of experience from actual physical presence.

The television coverage of the funeral itself seemed to mix a variety of other everyday film and television formats, narratives and

modes of address. It also articulated different temporalities, propos-
ing both synchronic and diachronic communities. Yet by being
broadcast live and uncut, it articulated three temporal planes as set
out by Scannell (1988). The steady progression of the funeral cortège
to Westminster Abbey, the continuous coverage of the service and
then the long drive north to Althorp all operated in 'clock-time', the
temporality of immediate experience. It also marked the end of an
individual 'life time' and was counterposed against the long *durée* of
institutional and generational time.

These three temporal planes can perhaps be accommodated under
Silverstone's heading of 'historical time', which is linear-durational,
progressive and irrecoverable (1983). This can be juxtaposed in the
television coverage of Diana's funeral by 'mythic time', which Silverstone describes as meaningful, cyclical and recoverable. In the
Princess of Wales's funeral, this 'mythic time' connoted antiquity and
the ever presence of God, monarch and country. Television, Silverstone argues, occupies mythic time. It is of a different temporal order
to everyday life. To switch on the television is to enter liminal space
and mythic time. As a result, what may have wielded a potent emotive force in the television coverage was the fact that an otherwise
mythical, cyclical and repetitive medium was depicting the irrecoverable, irreversible fact of death in historical time. Diana was dead.
She would no longer be on television.

Central to the princess's funeral, however, was ambiguity. As we
have seen, ambiguity also characterised the princess's status when she
was alive and when she died. Her death confounded expectations as
the narrative trajectory of her life radically altered from being a soap
opera to a tragedy, her personal news status from an important person to a victim. As we have argued, death is highly disruptive and can
lead to the breakdown of structures of meaning in the world. In the
immediate aftermath of her death, therefore, there emerged a period
of liminality which allowed for a variety of symbolic and practical
responses. On the day of the funeral, the liminality associated with
death was still present, although it had perhaps been alleviated to
some degree by responses that had become normative by the week's

end. The combination of this, the different genre and narrative formats, and the articulation of different temporalities meant that, in a sense, the live television coverage of the princess's death had liminal qualities. It occupied ambiguous place and time, 'betwixt and between', it marked a period of transition and transformation. That it was *deathly*, to use Mellencamp's term (1990), conformed to the very disturbing and potentially dangerous characteristics of liminality.

Yet the levels of disengagement expressed by some viewers suggest that not everyone experienced this as a liminal phenomenon. In this sense, the coverage may not have been liminal at all, but what Turner describes as quasi-liminal or liminoid (1978, 1982). The liminoid shares much in common with the liminal, such as separation from everyday life, the suspension of structures and hierarchies, even *communitas*. What marks it as separate is the exercise of free choice.

While liminality is dangerous, involving fear and duty, liminoid phenomena are predicated on choice, free will, and are not necessarily associated with danger. Such phenomena tend to be plural and fragmentary, and are prevalent in complex modern societies (1982). Liminoid phenomena, which can appeal to different groups, include various genres of leisure experience, in particular theatre, film, music and art (Turner, 1978, 1982). A typical liminoid experience, Turners argues, is a visit to the theatre where spectators engage in a range of experiences, emotions and ideas. They can occupy a range of subject positions and vicariously dabble with dangerous situations. Yet they will be able to return home safely at the end of the evening with their own world untouched. It is in this sense that we could describe the princess's funeral as a liminoid phenomenon. Some people may have had an intense emotional experience, but, at the end of the day, life returned to normal. What is clear, however, is that for some viewers it may have *seemed* liminal.

Notes

1. Source: BARB.
2. BBC 2 was a simulcast of BBC 1 output, but with subtitles for the deaf and hard of hearing. Channel 4 was the only terrestrial

broadcaster not to provide live coverage of the event, instead
scheduling programmes for children during the day.

3. Source: BARB. See also 'Overnight Ratings', *Broadcast*, 9
   September 1997, p. 2.

4. Several other authors have also referred to the establishment of co-
   temporal relations between unknown audience members in
   connection with a range of programming including public
   ceremonies (Bocock, 1974), televised films (Chaney, 1983), soaps
   (Scannell, 1996) and Diana's funeral (Davies, 1999).

5. A large survey in 1995 conducted by the Office for National
   Statistics found that women, irrespective of whether they were in
   paid employment or not, were likely to spend three and a half times
   as much time undertaking household tasks than men (Social Trends,
   1998).

6. The term 'Roman holiday' originates from a poem by Lord Byron
   referring to gladiatorial contests and has come to denote public
   spectacles and entertainment derived from death and injury. By
   ironic coincidence, *Roman Holiday* is also the title of a film (dir.
   William Wyler, 1953) about a princess who goes on holiday to Rome
   incognito and unwittingly spends her time with a member of the
   press.

5
After the Spectacle

The relationship between television and audience responses to the death of the Princess of Wales was profoundly complex. What quickly becomes clear is that the death of the princess and its consequences cannot be comprehended as a singular unitary event, but rather as a series of intricately interwoven events and processes. This is possibly the key to understanding some of the many conflicts and contradictions in both media and audience reactions that emerged in the days following that fatal car accident. The very ambiguous and complex nature of these events and the relationship of television to them would make an attempt at a conclusive summary a hazardous enterprise. Instead, by way of bringing this book to a close, it seems worthwhile reiterating or raising a few general points for thinking about responses to Diana's death and about television more generally.

One way to look at these events is to place them within the context of a range of media and social responses to other public and personal tragedies. In the first instance, the princess's death belongs to a canon of celebrity deaths of young, beautiful people such as James Dean (road accident), Jayne Mansfield (road accident) and Marilyn Munroe (suspected suicide). Perhaps presciently, Diana had herself attended the funeral of Princess Grace of Monaco (road accident) and, more recently, had been seen comforting a tearful Elton John at the funeral of Gianni Versace (shooting). Secondly, Diana's death also belongs to a canon of events involving public participation, such as the death of Princess Charlotte and her baby (1817), the sinking of the *Titanic* (1912) and the assassination in 1963 of J. F.

Kennedy (Davies, 1999). More recent examples, as Davies goes on to suggest, include the Hillsborough football stadium disaster (1989) and even, to a lesser extent, the Live Aid Concert (1984). Thirdly, at a socio-cultural level, the mourning responses to Diana's death, evident at the Hillsborough disaster and the shootings of schoolchildren at Dunblane (1996), incorporated personalised rites increasingly prevalent in contemporary funerary practice (Richardson, 1999). Fourthly, the media response to the princess's death was also predicated on journalistic practices and procedures which are conventionally used everyday, such as the use of vox pop, the use of dramatic images and the emphasis on conflict. Fifthly, the television response to the princess's death belongs to a particular genre of broadcast output, the 'disaster marathon' (Liebes, 1998) or 'catastrophe TV' (Mellencamp, 1990). The funeral itself belongs to a canon of televised 'media events' (Dayan and Katz, 1992, 1995), which have, in the United Kingdom, included the Coronation (1953), the funeral of Winston Churchill (1965) and the wedding of Diana and Prince Charles (1981).

What also characterises many of the social and media processes following the princess's death can be described as transformation or transgression. Transformation included the sudden shifts of narrative and media ontology on Diana's death from continuity to discontinuity; security to insecurity; reversibility to irreversibility; order to disorder. Boundaries were crossed and categories were changed. At a television news level, in Langer's terms (1998), a figure categorised as an important person was unexpectedly and dramatically transformed into a victim. In narrative terms, a continuous and long-running news and soap serial was radically closed and discontinued. Schedules were disrupted. Transgression characterised the apparent public response. People broke taboos to grieve in public. The mass display of such sentiment threatened the codes of expected behaviour and appeared to challenge the monarchy. In the streets, non-media people occupied media space and took centre stage in a reversal of media power (Couldry, 1999).

The apparent public response, however, should not necessarily be read as evidence of cultural change (Walter, 1999). Anthropologists, as Walter rightly suggests, have for a long time looked at how rules and hierarchies are reversed or undermined in certain social contexts. In this book, we have looked at the work of Victor Turner and seen that liminal periods such as emerged in the wake of the princess's death permit a variety of practical and emotional responses. Such responses, however, ultimately uphold social structures by establishing intense bonds within the social group. Other models for such social inversion include social catharsis where hierarchies are overturned to allow people to be 'king for a day', such as the Holi Festival in India where lower castes can throw water, dye and foodstuffs at those with higher social status (Marriot, 1966).

Another perspective is that such social movements implicitly restate established social rules (Eco, 1987). Taking as an example the Rabelaisian carnival examined in Bakhtinian metaphysics, Eco suggests that 'carnival can take place only once a year ... It takes a year of ritual observance for the violation of the ritual precepts to be enjoyed.' (1987, p. 275) Inversion of ordinary codes of behaviour reiterates the social order because 'the moment of transgression can exist only if a background of unquestioned observance exists' (ibid.). It was, therefore, against a background of grieving taboos and ordinary public inactivity and inertia that the response in the streets around London appeared abnormal and newsworthy. In Langer's terms, ordinary people were identified in television news as participating in something extraordinary (1998).

In the end, however, what may have made Diana's death so difficult for television to handle is that it constituted a moment of discontinuity for a medium that is, by its very nature, continuous. In this sense, as suggested by Silverstone (1983), television has certain temporal-mythic qualities. In Lévi-Strauss's analysis (1966), myth is set around irreconcilable oppositions that are never resolved. As Mary Douglas explains:

> According to Lévi-Strauss, the structure of myth is a dialectic structure
> in which opposed logical positions are stated, the oppositions mediated

by restatement, which again, when its internal structure becomes clear, gives rise to another opposition, which in its turn is mediated or resolved, and so on. (1967, p. 52).

Stories are worked and reworked, and different subject positions are occupied to show that extreme positions are 'untenable' (ibid., p. 59). This is also television's process. 'This can be likened to the process of "working-through" described by psychoanalysis, a process whereby material is not so much processed into a finished product as continuously worried over until it is exhausted' (Ellis, 1999, p. 55). In the end, therefore, '[t]elevision does not provide any overall explanation; nor does it necessarily ignore or trivialise. Television itself, just like its soap operas, comes to no conclusions. Its process of working-through is more complex and inconclusive than that' (ibid.). The difficulty the death of Diana presented, therefore, was that it was discontinuous, irrecoverable and conclusive.

Bibliography

Allen, R. C., 'Introduction', in R. C. Allen (ed.), *To Be Continued ... Soap Operas around the World* (London: Routledge, 1995).

Anderson, B., *Imagined Communities: Reflections on the Origin and Spread of Nationalism* (London: Verso, 1991).

Ang, I., *Watching Dallas: Soap Opera and the Melodramatic Imagination* (London: Routledge, 1985).

Ang, I., 'Melodramatic Identifications: Television Fiction and Women's Fantasy', *Living Room Wars: Rethinking Media Audiences for a Postmodern World* (London: Routledge, 1996).

Ariès, P., *Western Attitudes toward Death, from the Middle Ages to the Present* (London: Marion Boyars, 1976).

Aron, D. & S. Livingstone, 'A Media Event Interrupts the Global Soap Opera', *The Psychologist*, vol. 10 no. 11, 1997, pp. 501–2.

Augé, M., *Non-Places: Introduction to an Anthropology of Supermodernity* (London: Verso, 1995).

Barber, J. D., 'Peer Group Discussion and Recovery from the Kennedy Assassination', in B. S. Greenberg & E. B. Parker (eds), *The Kennedy Assassination and the American Public* (Stanford: Stanford University Press, 1965).

Bauman, Z., *Mortality, Immortality and Other Life Strategies* (Cambridge: Polity Press, 1992).

Becker, K., 'Media and the Ritual Process', *Media, Culture and Society*, vol. 17, 1995, pp. 629–46.

Becker, K., 'Ritual', *Screen*, vol. 39 no. 3, 1998, pp. 289–93.

Berger, P. & T. Luckmann, *The Social Construction of Reality* (Harmondsworth: Penguin, 1967).

Blackman, L., 'An *Extra*ordinary Life: The Legacy of an Ambivalence', *New Formations*, no. 36, 1999, pp. 111–24.

Bocock, R., *Ritual in Industrial Society: A Sociological Analysis of Ritual in Modern England* (London: George Allen & Unwin, 1974).

Bourdieu, P., *On Television and Journalism* (London: Pluto Press, 1998).

Bordwell, D. & K. Thompson, *Film Art* (New York: McGraw Hill, 1993).

Bowman, M., 'A Provincial City Shows Respect: Shopping and Mourning in Bath', in T. Walter (ed.), *The Mourning for Diana* (Oxford: Berg, 1999).

Bruner, J., 'Life as Narrative', *Social Research*, vol. 54, 1987, pp. 11–32.

Cardiff, D. & P. Scannell, 'Broadcasting and National Unity', in J. Curran, A. Smith & P. Wingate (eds), *Impacts and Influences: Essays on Media Power in the Twentieth Century* (London: Methuen, 1987).

Cathcart, F., 'For Whom the Bell Tolls', *The Psychologist*, vol. 10 no. 11, 1997, pp. 503–4.

Chaney, D., 'A Symbolic Mirror of Ourselves: Civic Ritual in Mass Society', *Media, Culture and Society*, vol. 5 no. 2, 1983, pp 119–35.

Corner, J., *Television Form and Public Address* (London: Arnold, 1995).

Couldry, N., 'Remembering Diana: The Geography of Celebrity and the Politics of Lack', *New Formations*, no. 36, 1999, pp. 77–91.

Davie, G. & D. Martin, 'Liturgy and Music', in T. Walter (ed.), *The Mourning for Diana* (Oxford: Berg, 1999).

Davies, D., 'The Social Facts of Death', in G. Howarth & P. C. Jupp (eds), *Contemporary Issues in the Sociology of Death, Dying and Disposal* (Basingstoke: Macmillan Press, 1996)

Davies, D., 'The Week of Mourning', in T. Walter (ed.), *The Mourning for Diana* (Oxford: Berg, 1999).

Dayan, D. & E. Katz, *Media Events: The Live Broadcasting of History* (Cambridge, Mass.: Harvard University Press, 1992).

Dayan, D. & E. Katz, 'Political Ceremony and Instant History', in A. Smith (ed.), *Television: An International History* (Oxford: Oxford University Press, 1995).

Day-Lewis, S., *One Day in the Life of Television* (London: Grafton Books, 1989).

Dixon, W. W., *Disaster and Memory: Celebrity Culture and the Crisis of Hollywood Cinema* (New York: Columbia University Press, 1999).

Doane, M. A., 'Ideology and the Practice of Sound Editing and Mixing', in E. Weiss & J. Belton (eds), *Film Sound: Theory and Practice* (New York: Columbia University Press, 1985).

Doane, M. A., 'Information, Crisis, Catastrophe', in P. Mellencamp (ed.), *The Logics of Television: Essays in Cultural Criticism* (London: BFI Publishing, 1990).

Douglas, M., 'The Meaning of Myth', in E. Leach (ed.), *The Structural Study of Myth and Totemism* (London: Tavistock Publications, 1967).

Durkheim, E., *The Elementary Forms of the Religious Life* (London: Allen & Unwin, 1915).

Eade, J. & M. J. Sallnow (eds), 'Introduction', *Contesting the Sacred: The Anthropology of Christian Pilgrimage* (London: Routledge, 1991).

Eco, U., 'The Comic and the Rule', *Travels in Hyperreality* (London: Picador, 1987).

Ellis, J., *Visible Fictions: Cinema, Television, Video* (London: Routledge, 1982).

Ellis, J., 'Television as Working-through', in J. Gripsrud (ed.), *Television and Common Knowledge* (London: Routledge, 1999).

Engel, G. L., 'Is Grief a Disease?', *Psychosomatic Medicine*, vol. 23, 1961, pp. 18–23.

Finnegan, R., '"Storying the Self": Personal Narratives and Identity', in H. Mackay (ed.), *Consumption and Everyday Life* (London: Sage, 1997).

Francis, D. et al., 'Kensington Garden: From Royal Park to Temporary Cemetery', in T. Walter (ed.), *The Mourning for Diana* (Oxford: Berg, 1999).

Gane, M., *Baudrillard's Bestiary* (London: Routledge, 1991).

Gauntlett, D. & A. Hill, *TV Living: Television, Culture and Everyday Life* (London: Routledge, 1999).

Geraghty, C., 'The Continuous Serial: A Definition', in R. Dyer et al. (eds), *Coronation Street* (London: BFI Publishing, 1981).

Geraghty, C., 'Story', *Screen*, vol. 39 no. 1, 1998, pp. 70–3.

Ghosh, P., 'Mediate and Immediate Mourning', in M. Merck (ed.), *After Diana: Irreverent Elegies* (London: Verso, 1998).

Giddens, A., *The Consequences of Modernity* (Cambridge: Polity Press, 1990).

Giddens, A., *Modernity and Self-Identity: Self and Society in the Late Modern Age* (Cambridge:

Polity Press, 1991).

Gray, A., 'Behind Closed Doors: Video Recorders in the Home', in H. Baehr & G. Dyer (eds), *Boxed In: Women and Television* (London: Pandora, 1987).

Gray, A., *Video Playtime: The Gendering of a Leisure Technology* (London: Routledge, 1992).

Harris, C., 'Secular Religion and the Public Response to Diana's Death', in T. Walter (ed.), *The Mourning for Diana* (Oxford: Berg, 1999).

Harvey, D., *The Condition of Postmodernity* (Oxford: Blackwell, 1989).

Hobsbawm, E., 'Introduction: Inventing Traditions', in E. Hobsbawm & T. Ranger (eds), *The Invention of Tradition* (Cambridge: Cambridge University Press, 1983).

Hobson, D., *Crossroads: The Drama of a Soap Opera* (London: Methuen, 1982).

Hockey, J., 'Women in Grief: Cultural Representation and Social Practice', in D. Field, J. Hockey & N. Small (eds), *Death, Gender and Ethnicity* (London: Routledge, 1997).

Horton, D. & R. R. Wohl, 'Mass Communication and Para-Social Interaction', *Psychiatry*, vol. 19, 1956, pp. 215–29.

Hughes-Freeland, F. & M. M. Crain (eds), 'Introduction', *Recasting Ritual: Performance, Media, Identity* (London: Routledge, 1998).

Independent Television Commission (ITC), *Television: The Public's View* (London: ITC Research, 1997).

Jordan, M., 'Realism and Convention', in R. Dyer et al. (eds), *Coronation Street* (London: BFI Publishing, 1981).

Kitzinger, J., 'Image', *Screen*, vol. 39 no. 1, 1998, pp. 73–9.

Langer, J., *Tabloid Television* (London: Routledge, 1998).

Lazarsfeld, P. F. & R. K. Merton, 'Mass Communication, Popular Taste and Organized Social Action', in W. Schramm (ed.), *Mass Communications* (Chicago: University of Illinois Press, 1972).

Lévi-Strauss, C., *The Savage Mind* (London: Weidenfeld & Nicholson, 1966).

Liebes, T., 'Television's Disaster Marathons: A Danger for Democratic Process?' in T. Liebes & J. Curran (eds), *Media, Ritual and Identity* (London: Routledge, 1998).

Lindemann, E., 'Symptomatology and Management of Acute Grief', in R. Fulton (ed.) *Death and Identity* (New York: John Wiley & Sons, 1965).

Livingstone, S., *Making Sense of Television: The Psychology of Audience Interpretation* (London: Routledge, 1998).

Lull, J., *Inside Family Viewing: Ethnographic Research on Television Audiences* (London: Routledge, 1990).

MacCabe, C., 'Realism and the Cinema: Notes on Some Brechtian Theses', *Screen*, vol. 15 no. 2, 1974, pp. 7–27.

MacCannell, D., *The Tourist: A New Theory of the Leisure Class* (New York: Schocken Books, 1989).

McKibbon, R., 'Mass-Observation in the Mall', in M. Merck (ed.), *After Diana: Irreverent Elegies* (London: Verso, 1998).

Marriot, M., 'The Feast of Love', in M. Singer (ed.), *Krishna Myths, Rites and Attitudes* (Honolulu: East-West Center Press, 1966).

Mellencamp, P., 'TV Time and Catastrophe: Or Beyond the Pleasure Principle of Television', in P. Mellencamp (ed.), *The Logics of Television: Essays in Cultural Criticism* (London: BFI Publishing, 1990).

Mellor, P. A., 'Death in High Modernity: The Contemporary Presence and Absence of Death', in D. Clark (ed.), *The Sociology of Death* (Oxford: Blackwell, 1993).

Merck, M. (ed.), After Diana: Irreverent Elegies (London: Verso, 1998)

Midwinter, E., *Out of Focus: Old Age, the Press and Broadcasting* (London: Centre for Policy on Ageing, 1991).

Mindak, W. H. & G. D.Hursch, 'Television's Functions on the Assassination Weekend', in B. S. Greenberg & E. B. Parker (eds), *The Kennedy Assassination and the American Public* (Stanford: Stanford University Press, 1965).

Morley, D., *Family Television: Cultural Power and Domestic Leisure* (London: Comedia, 1986).

Morrison, D., *Television and the Gulf War* (London: John Libbey, 1992).

Morse, M., 'The Television News Personality and Credibility: Reflections on the News in Transition', in T. Modleski (ed.), *Studies in Entertainment: Critical Approaches to Mass Culture* (Bloomington & Indiana: Indiana University Press, 1986).

Murdock, G., 'Thin Descriptions: Questions of Method in Cultural Analysis', in J. McGuigan (ed.), *Cultural Methodologies* (London: Sage, 1997).

Neale, S., 'Melodrama and Tears', *Screen*, vol. 27 no. 6, 1986, pp. 6–22.

O'Hear, A., 'Diana, Queen of Hearts: Sentimentality Personified and Canonised', in D. Anderson & P. Mullen (eds), *Faking It: The Sentimentalisation of Modern Society* (London: Social Affairs Unit, 1998).

Office for National Statistics, *Social Trends 28* (London: Office for National Statistics/HMSO, 1998).

Petrie, D. & J. Willis (eds), *Television and the Household: Reports from the BFI's Audience Tracking Study* (London: BFI Publishing, 1995).

Raphael, B., *When Disaster Strikes* (London: Hutchinson, 1986).

Richardson, R., 'Disposing with Diana: Diana's Death and the British Funerary Culture', *New Formations*, no. 36, 1999, pp. 21–33.

Scannell, P., 'Radio Times: The Temporal Arrangements of Broadcasting in the Modern World', in P. Drummond & R. Paterson (eds), *Television and its Audience* (London: BFI Publishing, 1988).

Scannell, P., *Radio, Television and Modern Life* (Oxford: Blackwell, 1996).

Schramm, W., 'Communication in Crisis', in B. S. Greenberg & E. B. Parker (eds), *The Kennedy Assassination and the American Public* (Stanford: Stanford University Press, 1965).

Sheatsley, P. B. & J. J. Feldman, 'A National Survey on Public Reactions and Behavior', in B. S. Greenberg & E. B. Parker (eds), *The Kennedy Assassination and the American Public* (Stanford: Stanford University Press, 1965).

Shevlin, M. et al., 'A Nation under Stress: The Psychological Impact of Diana's Death', in T. Walter (ed.), *The Mourning for Diana* (Oxford: Berg, 1999).

Shils, E. & M. Young, 'The Meaning of the Coronation', *Sociological Review*, vol. 1 no. 2, 1953, pp. 63–82.

Silverstone, R., 'The Right to Speak: On a Poetic for Television Documentary', *Media, Culture and Society*, vol. 5 no. 2, 1983, pp. 137–54.

Silverstone, R., *Television and Everyday Life* (London: Routledge, 1994).

Silverstone, R., 'Space', *Screen*, vol. 39 no. 1, 1998, pp. 81–4.

Sontag, S., 'The Imagination of Disaster', in G. Mast & M. Cohen (eds), *Film Theory and Criticism: Introductory Readings* (New York: Oxford University Press, 1974).

Street, E., 'Whose Princess Was She?' *The Psychologist*, vol. 10 no. 11, 1997, pp. 504–5.

Thompson, J. B., *Ideology and Modern Culture* (Cambridge: Polity Press, 1990).

Thompson, J. B., *The Media and Modernity: A Social Theory of the Media* (Cambridge: Polity Press, 1995).

Turner, V., *The Ritual Process: Structure and Anti-Structure* (Ithaca, New York: Cornell University Press, 1969).

Turner, V., 'Process, System and Symbol', *Daedalus*, vol. 106, 1977, pp. 61–80.

Turner, V. & E. Turner, *Image and Pilgrimage in Christian Culture: Anthropological Perspectives* (Oxford: Basil Blackwell, 1978).

Turner, V., *From Ritual to Theatre: The Human Seriousness of Play* (New York: PAJ Publications, 1982).

Vermorel, F. & J. Vermorel, *Starlust:* *The Secret Life of Fans* (London: Allen Lane, 1985).

Walter, T., 'The Mourning after Hillsborough', *Sociological Review*, vol. 39 no. 3, 1991, pp. 599–625.

Walter, T., J. Littlewood, & M. Pickering, 'Death in the News: the Public Invigilation of Private Emotion', *Sociology*, vol. 29 no. 4, 1995, pp. 579–96.

Walter, T., *On Bereavement: The Culture of Grief* (Buckingham: Open University Press, 1999a).

Walter, T. (ed.), 'The Questions People Asked', *The Mourning for Diana* (Oxford: Berg, 1999b).

Watson, J., 'The Structure of Chinese Funerary Rites', in J. Watson & E. S. Rawski (eds), *Death Ritual in Late Imperial and Modern China* (Berkeley: University of California Press, 1988).

Williams, R., *Marxism and Literature* (Oxford: Oxford University Press, 1977).

Williamson, J., 'A Glimpse of the Void', in M. Merck (ed.), *After Diana: Irreverent Elegies* (London: Verso, 1998).

Wilson, E., 'The Unbearable Lightness of Diana', in M. Merck (ed.), *After Diana: Irreverent Elegies* (London: Verso, 1998).

Index